The Vikings

Series edited by Paul Johnstone *and* Anna Ritchie

The VIKINGS

Michael Hasloch
Kirkby

PHAIDON · OXFORD
E. P. DUTTON · NEW YORK

Til en hvid fremmed fra Hordaland
Og til mørke fremmede fra Sjælland
Som sammen vakte i mig
En kærlighed til Norden.

Phaidon Press Limited, Littlegate House, St Ebbe's Street, Oxford
Published in the United States of America by E. P. Dutton & Co., Inc.

First published 1977

© 1977 Michael Kirkby

ISBN: hardback 0 7148 1718 X
       paperback 0 7148 1727 9
Library of Congress Catalog Card Number: 76-62639

Filmset in Great Britain by Keyspools Limited, Golborne, Lancashire

Printed in Italy by Amilcare Pizzi SpA, Milan

Contents

Foreword

Never has the Viking theme been more often rehearsed than in the last quarter of the twentieth century. The western world teems with 'Viking' clubs, pubs, cafés, ballrooms, floorshows, space probes—the list could doubtless be doubled without much effort.

In the field of more serious scholarship the bibliography of the Vikings has now become very extensive indeed. As always, research, particularly archaeological research, is an on-going process and is constantly adding to or modifying the already huge existing body of knowledge. Viking congresses and symposia are held and Viking societies issue their saga-books over a wider world than ever the Norsemen knew.

For a single, even polyglot, individual to keep abreast with all this would be humanly impossible, so would any attempt, even by a professional historian, to deal with the subject exhaustively in one short book. Though he has done intermittent service to Clio over the last forty years, 'professional historian' is a description to which the present writer would make no claim, and he has therefore approached the subject of the Vikings rather as one of their own saga-men might have done: 'in terms of men and women and human destiny, and in terms of a story'.

He is encouraged in this by the knowledge first, that neither a saga nor a modern history can ever be a perfect 'fixed and immutable record of known facts', because neither in the twelfth century nor the twentieth do human beings manage to write stripped of all prejudices and assumptions (they would be very dull if they did); and secondly, that over the centuries much of the most delightful and apparently respectable history turns out on analysis to be an arrangement of the facts in ways that happen to suit the writer—who could be more 'respectable' than Macaulay?

Men and women involved with the sort of intellectual activity that goes on in a university will pose questions like: 'Am I really sure this is accurate?' or 'Will this lay me open to correction?' before exposing their scholarship in print. Museum curators, of which the author is one, perhaps because they are often jacks of all trades, tend to be less inhibited. Along with creative writers and advertisers they are more likely to ask themselves: 'Does this (museum label, guide book, caption or whatever) really capture and convey what I'm trying to express to my public?' With a day-to-day obligation to interpret a vast miscellany of material objects to the widest possible cross-section of people, curators must of course use the fruits of many specialist researchers; but at the same time they are only too well aware that a bloodhound talent for unearthing new information is generally *not* combined in the same person with the artistry or synthesizing ability to make a historical subject acceptable to the general reader or viewer.

It is a plain and chastening fact that in a book like this much can only be touched on and much more is bound to be left unsaid. The author accepts his defects and omissions more readily for knowing that the reader with his curiosity about the Vikings still unassuaged has a number of better authorities, in many tongues, to turn to—Professors Arbman and Brøndsted in Denmark, Jones and Wilson in Britain, to name but four.

The Vikings (1961) by Holger Arbman, *The Vikings* (1965) by Johannes Brøndsted, *A History of the Vikings* (1968) by Gwyn Jones and *The Viking Achievement* (1970) by P. G. Foote and D. M. Wilson between them provide a thorough conspectus of the subject. Exhaustive bibliographies in these and other works are the guide to still deeper reading.

M. H. K.

Norway's fjord-indented coastline bred farmer/fishermen with the sea-going prowess to set out across the North Sea and the Atlantic in search of the farming land that was in such short supply at home.

Introduction

The Viking age is identified in most people's minds with Viking raids and the Viking raid has come to be thought of in terms of a nameless horde of pagans emerging out of the unknown, perpetrating its crimes and brutalities and slipping away once again into the dusk. But although this is certainly how it must have seemed to the immediate victims, the lapse of one thousand years has allowed us to make a more objective judgement. From various sources, but especially from the Vikings' own literature, we are now aware that these Scandinavian raiders came in the main from small well-organized communities of hard-working farmers and fishermen, and from a social background with a long continuous history: a society, in fact, which was not much less complex in its own way than the one which was being attacked. Far from coming in 'hordes', the raiders should probably be numbered in scores or hundreds at most. Nor is 'nameless' at all an appropriate epithet for a group in which each individual was well known to his fellows and distinguished by a name and a nickname, or a name and a family name, or sometimes all three. Indeed, as keen genealogists, most Vikings were able to rehearse their pedigrees over many generations. It is also worth reminding ourselves that even 'pagan' may not in every case be an accurate description: before the era of the major Viking raids began, Christian churches had been established in a number of places in Denmark (at least three of them known by name) and, whether Christian or pagan, in the settlements which the Vikings came from, firmly established standards of behaviour prevailed, broken only in the face of community disapproval and a rigid code of penalties. It was possible for figures like Olaf Tryggvason and Olaf Haraldsson (St. Olaf of Norway) to combine in one and the same person all the qualities of a Viking leader with those of an ardent and proselytizing Christian.

Without taking the analogy too far, a useful comparison can perhaps be made between Viking behaviour when on a raid, and the conduct of that

A leering face carved on the corner post of a sledge in the early days of Scandinavian expansion overseas captures some of the impertinent ferocity of the Viking raids.

twentieth century phenomenon and scourge, the football supporters' mob which not infrequently rampages through and terrorizes our cities. With a few criminal exceptions (which the Vikings also had), these mobs are composed in the main of individuals from perfectly respectable homes and settled family backgrounds, where such appalling language and behaviour or destructive activities would not for a moment be tolerated. Basically normal human beings—i.e. neither criminals nor pirates, except when they deliberately assume the role—the men who filled the Viking ships had that all-too-human attribute, a double standard of behaviour: one for the home and another for export only, or (as their present day pale imitators would put it) for the 'away match'.

Having said this, it is as well to admit that some of the manners and social arrangements of the Viking world were of the kind to bring out undesirable human traits. A society in which morality and religion (whether Christian or pagan) mould its growing children either superficially or not at all, and in which polygamy—even though not formally recognized—is widely practised, is all too likely, whether in the tenth or the twentieth century, to produce young people with an insufficiently stable background. Add to this an excessively masculine atmosphere, unsweetened by feminine values, and we can reasonably expect a rather large number of disturbed youths; willing recruits, first to adolescent gangs and later (perhaps by now inveterate delinquents) to the 'here' and its excesses of crime and violence.

Comparisons have been made between the Viking period of expansion from 800–1100 and the explosion of Islam in the century between 630–730. In some ways the Vikings were the same sort of catalyst in northern Europe that the Arabs had been in the Mediterranean 150 years earlier. But, although superficially alike, these outbursts of activity differ from each other in both cultural and religious aspects. The Scandinavian raiders, like their Germanic cousins before them, were eventually integrated with the people they conquered—people whose cultural life was in most respects not unlike their own. To the uncompromising monotheism of Mahomet, religious compromise was inconceivable: the holy war of Islam has been concerned down the centuries with the unconditional subjection of its conquered peoples, not their integration. By contrast, the loosely organized polytheism of the old Norse religion proved no great obstacle to the Vikings' transfer of allegiance from Odin to Christ. We shall see many individual examples of this.

In our attempts to trace a path through the labyrinth of Viking motivation and conduct there are two clues we shall do well to keep hold of. One is a certain opportunism and freedom from moral sanctions: if something can be had by force and for the taking, well and good; if not, the objective must be bargained and traded for. The other closely allied clue is the double standard of behaviour and character referred to earlier. These people really seem to have had the human faculty for switching from Jekyll to Hyde—and back again—unusually well developed. Bloody-minded pirates destroying all they could not carry off are transmuted within decades into law-abiding founding fathers of a settled agricultural community. Danelaw England in the late ninth century, Normandy in the early tenth and Iceland over both these periods are three places where one can see this transformation taking place. Over shorter time spans this process was reflected in the changing role of a Dane, Norwegian or Icelander in his own homeland. One Spring a chieftain may decide to sail abroad and go raiding for booty; in the next the saga shows him walking out with a seed-basket in one hand (and a sword in the other!) to sow his cornfield. Since crime and violence have always been more news-worthy than peaceful pursuits the Vikings were bound to become memorable as sowers of destruction rather than as broadcasters of corn: nevertheless, it was in the latter role not the former that their lasting and significant contribution has been made.

Raiding and its civilized sister trading are by their very nature ephemeral activities. For all the vastness of their field of operations the permanent achievements of the Rus, the largely Swedish warrior-merchants in the East, have always remained difficult to assess. In the comparatively tiny lands of England and Normandy the Dano-Norwegian settlements have changed the whole history of western Europe and, eventually, of the world. It is for this reason (rather than simply because the author is English!) that so large a part of this brief account of the Vikings is devoted to these countries.

Chapter I   **Viking York**

Our opening scene is the city of York, unrivalled capital since the year AD 71 of the northern parts of Britain, and second only to that other Roman city also situated on a North Sea estuary—London.

York and London indeed had much in common. Both are sited with that unerring eye for 'the opportunities of places' (as the Roman historian Tacitus puts it) on tidal rivers at similar distances from the open sea. The situations of both were chosen because they represented the lowest convenient bridging points of the rivers Ouse and Thames respectively and each took advantage of higher ground rising above the surrounding marshland. In the case of York this consisted of a ridge of glacial deposits connecting to the east with the range of chalk hills now called the Wolds, and to the west with the Pennine range and thus eventually with the Irish Sea. York's choice of situation was so apposite that it has remained a centre of communications and the site of the Northern Command in this island from that day to this.

Just as in Londinium the Fleet brook formed a serviceable moat and shipping creek to the west of the Roman fortress, so in York the beck or small river Foss gave merchant vessels useful access to the civilian suburb occupying the marshy ground between its sluggish course and the eastern (or more properly south-eastern) wall of Eburacum. For Roman 'York' was made up of three clearly defined districts: the legionary fortress itself with massive stone walls dating from the third and fourth centuries, the *colonia* or chartered settlement which formed a bridgehead on the opposite bank of the Ouse, and lastly the civilian suburbs scattered round the walls of the fortress, including the narrow strip between the riverfront defences and the Ouse bank.

Eburacum was as splendid a town as any in the western Empire. For some years in the third century the emperors Severus and Caracalla had held their courts in its *domus palatina* or palace; in the fourth century the emperor Constantius had died in York and his son Constantine the Great been proclaimed there. The majestic scale of its *principia*, residence of the imperial governors, is evident from the 27-foot high Doric columns, one of which was re-erected on the 1900th anniversary (1971) of the city's foundation. Part of the S.W. corner tower of the Roman fortress is still standing.

During the early fifth century York's function as administrative capital and legionary fortress of the Roman Empire was dwindling. Even while the Roman troops and civil servants were still functioning, people from the opposite shores of the North Sea had been filtering into the city and its neighbourhood, at first by invitation as mercenaries and servants—several cremation cemeteries around York have yielded Anglian urns from this period. But before long these foreigners were coming in increasing numbers as settlers on their own account: 'In a short time', says Bede, 'the people of the newcomers began to increase so much that they became a source of terror to the very natives who had invited them.'

The genius of these Germanic and Scandinavian people (who eventually inherited most of the Roman Empire) dwelt essentially in farms, villages and small communities. On the whole they seem to have avoided the massive buildings, walls and even roads of Roman civilization. In our examination of post-Roman York (it was a site too strategic to lapse altogether) it will therefore be with the *colonia* and suburbs rather than with the fortress itself that we shall mainly be concerned. When we come to the near-amphibious Vikings we can expect those areas with the readiest access to the rivers Ouse and Foss to yield most of the archaeological evidence.

In the case of York and northern England the Viking invasions represent merely the second, rather dramatic, phase of a much more prolonged Nordic settlement. To understand the situation at their arrival (866) it is therefore necessary to take a brief look at the four intervening centuries of settlement and civilization under their Anglian predecessors.

Who were these Angles? We have no reason to doubt Bede, a careful and accurate historian, when he says that the East Angles (Norfolk and Suffolk), Middle Angles (Leicestershire and south Lincolnshire), Mercians (Worcestershire, Staffordshire and Derbyshire) and the entire Northumbrian stock (i.e. all those living north of the Humber) came originally 'from the country called Angulus . . . between the provinces of the Jutes and the Saxons'. King Alfred, another very truthful person, and one steeped in English historical traditions, confirms this when he inserts into Ohthere's narrative the specific information that what is now S. Jutland and N. Slesvig formed the original home of the Angles—the latter still has a district called Angeln. Once the confusion of the initial invasion period is over, Anglian and Saxon archaeological material can be clearly distinguished. The fact that the Angles came from Scandinavia has an important bearing on the Viking settlements in England 400 years later.

The 27-foot high columns of a Roman imperial residence (left) lay in impressive ruin when the Vikings first entered York. This one (above) came to light again during excavations beneath the Minster in 1969. Topped by a later arcade of medieval windows, a corner tower of York's Roman fortress still stands (below).

About York itself during the sixth century scarcely anything is known, though there is geological evidence that its site may have been subject to severe flooding. In this nameless, dateless era of the Dark Ages all we can be certain of is that year after year boatloads with families, clans and whole tribes were settling among the native British, sometimes dispossessing them, sometimes cultivating new clearings alongside them. An example of this tribal settlement is revealed by place-names: a people called the Hrype who occupied a tract of land on the rivers Ure and Nidd left their name in Ripon, Ripley, Great and Little Ribston, and so on.

For waterborne immigrants like the Angles these and the other tributaries of the Humber offered the obvious means of access to the territory which subsequently became Yorkshire. The resident British gave these Anglian settlers the collective name *Dere* and when around 550 they organized themselves into a kingdom the name Dera or Deira 'land of rivers' was retained. (It survived in Derawudu and Derafeld, the old names for Beverley and Driffield). The northern section of Northumbria, from the Tees to the Firth of Forth, was named Bernicia.

York (its Anglian inhabitants were now calling it Eoforwic) clearly remained the most important place, not only in Deira but in the whole of northern Britain. For this reason Gregory I, the pope who in 597 sent St. Augustine with the first mission to the island, gave instructions in 601 that as soon as possible York should be an independent archbishopric, equal to Canterbury. In doing this the Pope would also be aware that Eburacum had been a Christian bishopric since 314—indeed it is quite possible that a Christian congregation, if not an actual church, still survived in York from Roman times.

This splitting by Gregory of the country's ecclesiastical government also stressed its secular division; indeed the distinction between the English peoples north and south of the Humber profoundly affected their early history and has not ceased to do so to this day.

St. Augustine and his missionaries entered Britain from the south and, before they could make contact with Northumbria, had to overcome the active heathendom of Wessex and its neighbours. For the real stronghold of paganism in this island was not the north, but rather the areas of Saxon settlement in the south and south-east. Although pagan temples certainly existed in Northumbria, no heathen place-names seem to have survived, whereas, in Wessex, place-names from heathen sanctuaries are numerous.

It was not therefore until 625–7 that one of Augustine's colleagues, Paulinus, was able to carry out the papal instructions of 601 by re-establishing the bishopric of York, building a new church and baptizing Edwin the Northumbrian king inside it. However, Paulinus made up for lost time and in the next six years was dipping converts in all the rivers of Edwin's territory, from the Tweed in Bernicia to the Trent down in Lindsey—of which little kingdom Edwin was then overlord.

From Edwin's death in 632 till about 700 the focus of Northumbria was in Bernicia rather than Deira, and in this period it was the monks of the Celtic church rather than priests from Rome who carried on the conversion of the North, working from such centres as Lindisfarne and Monkwearmouth.

In the eighth century, however, the Northumbrian focal point moved permanently south again and York became fully and finally re-established as the civil and religious capital of Northumbria. More than this, it now gained international recognition as a centre not just of English but of west European culture. During the 730's Egbert, brother of the king of Northumbria became archbishop of York. He was a friend of Bede, a writer and founder of the cathedral school and library; he was also the instructor and patron of Alcuin, England's first internationally known scholar and educationist. Alcuin lived in York till 781 when he became educational adviser to Charlemagne, whom he met on his return journey from Rome.

The late eighth century was about the first opportunity for west Europeans to travel peacefully and pursue international scholarship and correspondence since the reign of Constantine 450 years earlier. But it is a portent of events to come that by 793—the last time Alcuin visited York—he was already complaining that the violence of pagans deterred him from returning to his native land. 'What should I do in Northumbria?' he asks, 'where no-one is free from fear.' The grounds of Alcuin's complaint were partly the Viking raids then just beginning and partly the unsettled condition of Northumbria in the late eighth century. At this time the dominant state in England was Mercia under its powerful king Offa (757–96); during Offa's reign Northumbria had no less than seven rulers, most of whom came to a violent end.

By the year 830, however, Mercia as well as Northumbria had submitted to the rising power of Wessex, whose supremacy was achieved just in time to form the basis of English resistance to the Viking onslaught of 835 onwards. Looking with hindsight we can surmise that, failing this supremacy, the whole of England, not just part of it, could well have become a 'Danelaw'. In this event the country would very likely have permanently remained a Scandinavian nation with Germanic minorities, rather than the other way round, and Canute the Great's North Sea Empire might have survived to this day.

The stubborn resistance of the Saxons between 835 and 878 had the effect of diverting the Danish Vikings towards those Anglian areas of England whose inhabitants might be expected to offer them a more sympathetic reception. Attacks on Northumbria had certainly begun by 844, but, as there is for this period no northern equivalent of the Anglo-Saxon Chronicle, our historical evidence is limited. Nor is there much help from archaeology. There have been many scattered finds of small metal objects and a quantity of fragments of stone memorial crosses. The most

The stump of a stone cross (left), the bronze tip of a scabbard (above right) and a tiny pewter brooch (left) are among many things recently excavated at York that were decorated in the interlacing Danish style that Viking settlers in England developed in the 10th century.

important of these were found in the Christian cemetery occupying what is now the south transept of York Minster.

But on the whole York seems singularly lacking in archaeological evidence throughout the Anglian period, considering its known importance as a royal and ecclesiastical centre. For example, the cathedral church of St. Peter (on the site of the Roman *principia* and where the present Minster stands) had been often enlarged and embellished since its foundation in 627, and by Alcuin's time must have been quite a lofty structure containing a bell-tower and about 30 altars. Yet excavations have been able to shed little light on its actual design, and the same is true of the other churches in Anglian York, all of which were in the suburbs or old *colonia* area, not the fortress.

Some indication of Northumbria's relative decline in the ninth century comes from coins. First a copper issue (modelled on the coinage of Mercia) replaced the gold and silver coinage previously minted by the archbishops and Northumbrian kings: then during the 850's even this ceased to be issued. In 865–6, after a reign of 18 years king Osberht was deposed in favour of a ruler 'of the royal seed' called Aella. Northumbria was therefore in a state of civil discord and York itself probably undefended when the Danish army, mounted on horses bought (or stolen) in East Anglia, suddenly arrived there in the autumn of 866, under the leadership of Ingvar, Ubba and Halfdan. According to the chroniclers they laid waste everything up to the mouth of the Tyne and, on the 1st of November, occupied the city of York and made it their winter quarters.

Next spring, reconciled in the face of this common enemy, Osberht and Aella joined forces and, on the 21st of March, 867, launched a counter attack on the Northumbrian capital. A graphic account of this Battle of York, one of the most momentous local conflicts in English history, is given by the chronicler Symeon of Durham, drawing on early sources. From this it appears that the greater part of the Northumbrian forces perished, including the two leaders, Osberht and Aella, also that the walls of the Roman fortress of Eburacum were still in a condition to be a significant factor in the struggle for the city.

Deira and Bernicia thus passed from Anglian into Danish Viking control. In York itself, and in Deira, there seems to have been an interregnum between the death of king Osberht in 867 and the return in 875 of Halfdan as the first Viking king. In Bernicia however, three Anglian rulers—Egbert, Ricsige and then another Egbert were given nominal control during the first decade after the Danish conquest (867–77). During much of this time archbishop Wulfhere absented himself from his cathedral city and went to Mercia.

After subjugating—but not at this point occupying—Northumbria, the Great Army withdrew southwards to carry on its campaign against Wessex. It did not return in strength till 875–6. This time only part of the army, under its leader Halfdan, returned north, while another part occupied East Anglia.

It was this splitting away of perhaps two-thirds of the Scandinavian forces into Anglian territory that enabled the Saxons under their young king Alfred to win the decisive victory of 878 and to repel the remaining Viking forces for ever from Wessex and south-east England.

Without any doubt 876 marked the turning point in the whole Viking campaign against England. This was the year in which the Danish Vikings ceased to be the first and foremost fighting men and predators and instead made settlement of the land their first priority. Much of Northumbria seems to have been shared out among the Viking soldiers under the direct supervision of Halfdan; the chronicler also states that 'part of his army rebuilt the city of York, cultivated the land in its neighbourhood and settled there'. This may refer to the repairing of the city wall.

On their arrival in Northumbria most of the Vikings will have been pagans. Their ready acceptance of Christianity at the hands of archbishop Wulfhere (who had returned to York in about 873) and his fellow-priests will have been an important factor in this settlement. This apparently speedy conversion implies some degree of encouragement of the rank and file by their leaders. If so, this is quite in line with the conversion of other Viking peoples. When Christianity (a century or more later) was adopted as the national religion in Denmark, Norway, Kiev-Novgorod and Iceland, it was as the result of political or royal decisions.

King Halfdan, however, belonged to an earlier generation of the Danish royal house, and was undoubtedly a pagan. Symeon of Durham relates that, because of his sins against the church (destruction of monasteries and partitioning of church lands among the soldiers), 'the wrath of God came upon him so that he began to putrefy and stink and, his whole army casting him out, he fled by sea.' Some authorities think that this first king of Denmark and Northumbria died in Ireland around 877 on a retributive raid against Ivar of Dublin who had been claiming authority over the Norse settlers in N.W. England and attacking neighbouring Strathclyde. Symeon places Halfdan's death in 882, the year that York's first Christian Viking king, Guthfrith Hardaknutsson, began his 14-year reign.

Even before the Norman conquest a mass of legends had gathered around Guthfrith, and the fact that these were current in Scandinavia as well as in England lends some evidence to the strange story of his election to the Northumbrian kingship.

Symeon relates the tradition that the abbot of Carlisle was commanded in a dream to go over to the Danish army camped on the Tyne, find the young orphan Guthfrith, redeem him from bondage and proclaim him king, all of which he duly did: 'and the King himself and the whole army swore peace and faithfulness as long as they lived; and this oath they duly kept.' Guthfrith is a name with ancient, and indeed royal, associations in Scandinavia where royal exiles were not infrequently rescued from obscurity for a glorious future. Even if only partly true, the story throws rather a different light on these Danish Vikings from the lurid glow in which they are traditionally bathed. Guthfrith's reign may indeed have been a time of comparative peace and prosperity for York and for Northumbria. Certainly coins were minted again at York; a hoard found at Cuerdale near Preston includes many with the names of king Knut (this royal Danish name may have been Guthfrith's cognomen) and king Sigefrid who was probably Guthfrith's successor from 894–7.

Despite their oaths of 'peace and faithfulness' and their ready adoption of Christianity, and despite further oaths of allegiance to king Alfred, it would be unrealistic to suppose that the Danish settlers in York and Northumbria were immediately transformed thereby into full supporting citizens of the English state. When it came to taking sides, the Danes' instinctive loyalties were still first and foremost with their fellow countrymen and against the forces of Wessex. There is no doubt that the uncertain loyalties of Northumbria, East Anglia and the whole Danelaw helped to protract the struggle with the Vikings which occupied the end of Alfred's reign.

But, on the other hand, it is equally certain that from Guthfrith's reign onwards an increasing degree of supremacy was being established by Alfred and his successors over the Danish kings of York. This process continued after 919 when the Danish line was ousted by more stirring rulers of the Norse dynasty from Dublin, the first of these being Raegnald Guthfrithsson who for some years previously had been operating in northern Northumbria. Raegnald's successor Sihtric not only acknowledged the suzerainty of Wessex but married king Athelstan's sister.

No complete or continuous history of Northumbrian affairs exists for the troublous period which intervened between the reign of Sigefrith and the last reign of Eirik Bloodaxe, the final Scandinavian ruler of York—that is, from around 900 to 954. If such a record ever did exist it has not survived, and the political history of York as capital city of Scandinavian Northumbria is consequently obscure and conjectural. This is what renders the evidence of archaeology so important for the period—every scrap of information it can give is vital in a time when historical records shed so little light.

In fact during the first half of the tenth century even the conventional division of history into reigns is hardly appropriate for York, so rapid are the permutations and so little is known beyond the mere names of the rulers. Of the Viking 'kings' of Northumbria, only 5 reigned until their deaths, and of these, 3 were killed in battle. In the teeth of historical and (as yet) archaeological inadequacy a study of the three-quarters of a century when York was the (relatively) independent capital of Viking Scandinavia yields three general observations. The scope of these ranges from west European significance down to merely local. First, this was genuinely one of those periods of prolonged uncertainty when events on a national scale could have turned out quite differently from the way in which they actually did—given that, in retrospect, all historical events are inevitable.

For what could have taken place between 876 and 954 was the fusion of York and Dublin into a single Viking state stretching from Ireland across the Irish Sea, with the Isle of Man, across the waist of Britain between Dee and Solway, and thence across the North Sea towards the Viking homelands themselves. Such a union with its mixed Anglo-Viking and Celtic population would have isolated the Saxon nation to the south of it from all the peoples in Britain to the north of it, with lasting effects both on our island story and on the subsequent development of Scandinavia as well. The tactic which did most to break up the York-Dublin axis from east to west was the steady establishment by the West Saxon kings of burhs or fortified towns from the south to the north of England.

Secondly, at the regional level, the Vikings, as one of the great trading peoples in all history, expanded York during the period of their rule from its traditional role of military garrison and administrative centre into that of a busy mercantile port. In varying degrees this activity will have affected the whole region—the northern Danelaw, of which York was the metropolis; it may legitimately be regarded as one of the factors in the subsequent

The York-Dublin axis.

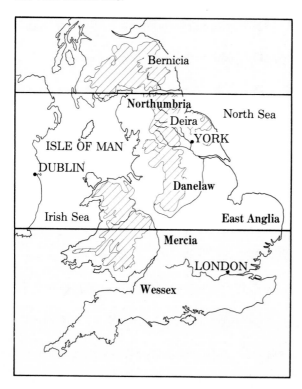

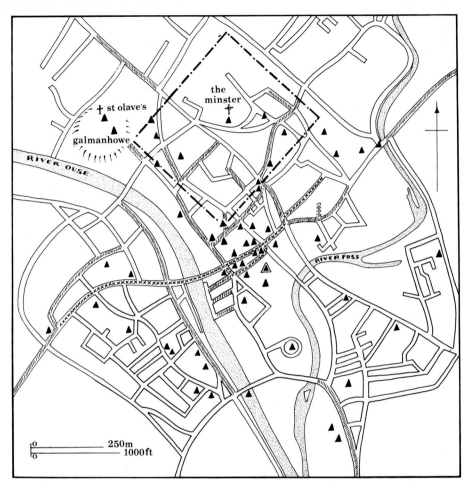

Viking York. Streets with names of Scandinavian origin (shaded) show where the Vikings settled; the main artery (with crosses) runs to one side of the Roman fortress (square outline). Viking finds (plain triangles) have so far been concentrated at the confluence of the two rivers; the 1976 excavation (outlined triangle) revealed an abundance of material in ground sloping down to the Foss water-front.

development of this zone as the nation's chief commercial bloc, containing as it still does a disproportionately high number of its major ports and manufacturing cities.

Thirdly, on the more local scale, there is no doubt that the layout of York itself was radically altered by the Viking invasions and settlement since its 'Scandinavianizing' was more thorough and lasting than that of any other English town. The evidence for this is twofold: one part comes from a study of the Viking place-names and street names, many of which are still in use, and the other from the archaeological material of the tenth and eleventh centuries found in and around those places and streets; bearing in mind that,

23

as far as dating is concerned in a period as recent as 876–954, the radiocarbon method is not very valuable; the margin of error is so large one can generally only say 'Early Viking' or 'Late Viking'.

York differed from most other Viking trading centres in that it was an outgrowth, or attachment to an ancient existing city. Thus the main artery of the Scandinavian settlement ran to one side of the still-surviving Roman fortress whose pillared buildings, walls and interval towers of gleaming Tadcaster stone represented a totally different world from the timber and shingle shanty-town that was growing up along the banks of Ouse and Foss.

Most of the streets and lanes in York have the suffix 'gate' (Old Scandinavian *gata* 'street') or 'gale' (Scandinavian *geil* 'a narrow passage between houses') and in these names much of the history of Viking York can be traced, together with the occupations of its inhabitants.

One of the first streets built may have been Bretgate (now Jubbergate) the street where the Bretar or Britons lived: Celtic inhabitants of Cumbria brought to York by the Dublin Vikings, perhaps in a servile capacity. Micklegate is the 'great street', Ousegate the road leading down to the river Ouse. Coppergate is the street of the wrights (Old Scandinavian *koppari*), Skeldergate, the street of the shieldmakers (*skjaldari*).

Outside the north-west walls of the fortress is Bootham, 'at the booths'—or market stalls, Feasegate (originally Feasegale) is the lane of the *fe-hus* or cow house and Fishergate the fishermen's street. In Haver Lane, Hungate and Swinegate were goats, dogs and pigs respectively.

Stonegate, on the line of the *via principalis* of the legionary fortress, still had its Roman stone paving, unlike the Anglian and Viking roads outside the Roman city, which must often have been ankle-deep in mud, or at best lined with duckboards.

The kings and later earls of Northumbria may have had one of their residences on the rising ground called Galman's how or hill where Siward built a church and dedicated it to St. Olaf of Norway (now St. Olave's). The Scandinavian personal name Galman is itself a link between York and Viking Dublin being a form of the Old Irish name Colman.

But, though they found themselves in a city context, the Vikings of York were only in an incidental sense 'citizens'. First and foremost they were international merchants, traders, shipmen and artisans making use of an ideal site on which a former civilization happened to have left behind a city. And so it is not in the well-drained Roman fortress with its elaborate stone sewers, but in the crowded squalor of the surrounding marshes that the archaeologist of Viking York mainly directs his search. The buildings he is looking for do not stand on masonry footings but on timber ground-sills, and have planked floors, and walls of stout vertical planking (staves) sometimes solid and sometimes interlaced with horizontal osiers.

The artefacts which archaeologists have discovered and will continue to discover in and around these cabins are, in the main, either simple domestic

*St Olave's church in York was founded by
Siward, Knut's appointee to the earldom of
Northumbria. A ninth-century coin struck
at York bears St Peter's name on one side
and this Viking dagger on the other.*

things: combs, pins, wooden spoons, scrapers, bone-skates, or the relics of whatever trades and occupations were carried on inside them—mainly those on which everyday life depends, like weaving, grinding corn, blacksmithing or leatherworking. One site revealed that the tanners and workers were living, not even in timber huts, but in flimsy wattle and daub structures, which even then were riddled with woodworm and death-watch beetle. The floors were covered with chicken-dung and the workshops must have crawled with maggots, which thrived on the rotting animal refuse.

It is to the waterlogged state of Viking York that much of the excavated material—leather, wood, cloth fragments—owes its preservation. Some of the textiles equal examples found in Scandinavia, and by examination with the electron-microscope it has even been possible to determine the type of sheep from which their wool came. Pottery and glass are of course not dependent on these conditions for their survival; the long narrow river-frontages on Skeldergate have yielded an excellent series of Anglo-Scandinavian pottery, but little glass has been found in Viking York. Coinage has already been referred to: one ecclesiastical issue with the name of St. Peter nevertheless bears on it a Viking dagger. Several anonymous coinages—lacking the name of king or archbishop—seem to have been issued in the northern Danelaw during the Viking period.

In 1976, exactly eleven hundred years after 876 when the Vikings first gave settlement priority over warfare in Northumbria, a major two-year archaeological excavation was inaugurated right in the heart of Viking York. The prediction was that finds of international significance would be made—finds expected to be amongst the most important of the Viking period ever discovered on a British site.

The area concerned, consisting of some 1,500 square metres, lies between Coppergate and the river Foss and is believed to be in the middle of the Viking trading settlement. Commenting on the excavation, its director said: 'We expect this outstandingly important excavation to capture the public imagination. Viking York was unique, the archaeological site is large, and local waterlogging will have successfully protected a whole range of material both man-made and organic. Our most valuable finds will reflect trading and craft working rather than war-mongering, for Viking York was the prosperous and settled centre for the whole of Yorkshire.'

Under its Danish and Norse kings Viking regional sovereignty survived in York later than anywhere else in England. Even after the expulsion of Eirik Bloodaxe in 954, York and the northern Danelaw remained overwhelmingly Scandinavian in population and sympathies. It was to York that the body of England's first Danish king, Svein, was carried for burial in 1014 and, over half a century later, Anglo-Scandinavian support for the Norwegian bid for the English throne nearly changed the fateful events of 1066.

Chapter II **The Viking World**

'Addicted to, or living by, plunder; plundering, marauding, thieving, destructive—preying on others'—*predatory* is the single adjective which sums up what the world at large has thought and for the most part still thinks about the Vikings between 770 and 1070 in their Age of Expansion.

Whether in the world of men or of animals the relationship of the victim to his predator has always contained a strong element (encouraged by the latter) of terror. Some of this terror is caused by the suddenness of the attack; more often it is the result of a fear of the great unknown from which the predator emerges. But follow the lion to his den and watch him play with his cubs—see our Viking warrior back in his village being scolded by his wife—and some at least of our terror is dispelled.

Provided one is not too closely identified with the victim, familiarity with the 'off duty' background and circumstances of the predator may breed not necessarily contempt but rather a degree of understanding and fellow feeling from which a more balanced assessment of the situation can emerge—a situation fairly aptly described in W. S. Gilbert's much-sung verses:

> When a felon's not engaged in his employment
> Or maturing his felonious little plans
> His capacity for innocent enjoyment
> Is just as great as any honest man's
>
> When the enterprising burglar's not a-burgling
> When the cut-throat isn't occupied in crime—
> He loves to hear the little brook a-gurgling
> And listen to the merry village chime.

To understand all is not always to forgive all—with the Vikings that would indeed be a counsel of perfection. But a knowledge of their context, background and motivation cannot but widen our appreciation of and sympathy for them as suffering fellow human-beings in a difficult and adverse world; and of a people who, whether we like them or not, did much to mould the society we have inherited today. These are the main reasons for this chapter's exploration of the Viking homelands during the centuries just before and just after the beginning of the Christian era.

The Scandinavian setting

Throughout human history, poverty and adversity (provided they are not of an overwhelming kind) have been the traditional stimuli of successful and famous careers and in a collective sense the physical nature of the Scandinavian world at this time was certainly one of the main incentives behind the Viking success story. If you could survive a childhood of Norwegian winters you could face anything life might send thereafter.

The conditions and climate were, of course, largely a question of latitude. Tucked away at the north-west corner of the huge Asiatic land mass, Scandinavia begins (southern Denmark) just south of latitude 55° and ends (northern Norway) north of 70°; Iceland is bisected by the 65th parallel. We shall gain some idea of the distances involved if we remember that Copenhagen is nearer to Rome than it is to the North Cape. Thus, by reason of its latitudes, Scandinavia was the part of western Europe where the ice cap reigned longest and deepest. When early Stone Age man was beginning to colonize further south in the European continent, much of Scandinavia still remained uninhabitable. Indeed its landscape, a legacy of the ice age, has always presented its human inhabitants, including the Vikings, with a challenge and inspiration rather than with any soft options. Even today no traveller in these lands can forget the ice age's continuing effect on the terrain: the huge surviving glaciers in Norway and Iceland, the stupendous fjords gouged from the ancient Norwegian rocks, the undulating moraines and the thousand lakes of Sweden and the boulder sands and clays deposited by the melting glaciers over the whole face of Denmark. Owing to the relative poverty of much of these soils, farming in the lands facing the North Sea and the Baltic has never been easy. Across Skåne and Denmark the 'slash and burn' method used by the earliest farming communities left a trail of burnt forests in their wake.

By the New Stone Age (3000 BC) the peoples of the north had made up for their comparatively late start. The most suitable soils for neolithic agriculture in southern Sweden, Denmark and Slesvig were those provided by the most recently deposited moraines. From the quantity of implements of native flint that has survived and from their impressive size and workmanship it is clear that during the Neolithic period southern Scandinavia supported a rich culture. This continued to flourish through the subsequent Bronze Age when wonderful objects were produced both in that

Played in pairs, perhaps in processions, about 50 of these horns have been found in Denmark dating from the Bronze Age.

metal and in gold. From Danish butter packets most housewives of today are familiar with the massive and unique bronze *lurs* or trumpets; to listen to these—or replicas of them—blown in matched pairs at some modern ceremonial occasion is to hear the authentic voice of the lively and powerful civilization which flourished in the Viking lands almost two thousand years before they themselves entered the Scandinavian scene.

But around 1000 BC the northern lands entered a period of decline. The climate, which had been comparatively dry and warm, became colder, wetter and less sunny. Life, especially during the long and often hungry winter darkness, became harder—the archaeological remains from this period are both poorer and rarer.

From about 600 BC onwards, moreover, the stage of western Europe, including Britain, was occupied by a vigorous and warlike people, having the use of iron weapons. These Celts spread themselves, their culture and the branches of their language, from the Rhine to the Mediterranean. During this Celtic Iron Age the northern lands became a backwater and remained so when the Celts were themselves engulfed by a still greater power, that of Rome. Nothing so much differentiates the culture of the Vikings' own homelands from that of the lands they invaded as the fact that all the latter (apart from Ireland and the Atlantic islands) had come under the rule of the Roman Empire whereas they themselves had not been thus absorbed. During these centuries—the first four of the Christian era—there were of course contacts between Scandinavia and the Empire and rich imports of gold, silver, bronze and glass in exchange for furs, walrus-ivory, amber and slaves; imports, above all, of gold and silver coinage. Is not the öre, the monetary unit of Scandinavia, derived from the Latin *aureus*?

'Out of the north shall all evils come'—says the prophet Jeremiah, and even before the Roman Empire the movement of the peoples out of Scandinavia had begun to harass their southern neighbours. Republican armies before 100 BC had encountered the Ambrones from Amrum and the north Frisian islands, also the Cimbri and the Teutones, both of whom originally hailed from northern Jutland. Later, during the years of the Empire when the power of the Celts was waning, the wandering of the northern peoples and their impact on more peaceable lands to the south were both intensified.

Indeed, one can look at the classical 'Viking Period' of 770 to 1070 as the last phase (until the nineteenth-century emigrations) of a much longer Scandinavian expansionist movement, one that was certainly already under way in the darkest of Dark Ages: when the Goths left eastern Sweden to settle in the Baltic provinces and the Langobards left southern Sweden to make their settlements (e.g. Bardowick) down the Elbe and finally land up, as Lombards, in northern Italy; when the Burgundar (perhaps) forsook their Baltic island of Bornholm and migrated through Germany to central Gaul and our own Angles vacated the sandy wastes of Slesvig in favour of more fertile lands in eastern Britain. So thoroughgoing, according to Bede, was this the last emigration that 'the country which is now called Angulus (now Angeln) is said to have remained uninhabited from that day to this. Despite the tempting similarity of name, the Jutes almost certainly did not arrive in Britain direct from Jutland but were a Germanic people from the mouths of the Rhine.

All these migratory activities were comparable with those that were about to take place several centuries later in the Viking Age proper. With 'a prow at each end' (Tacitus) and with their dragon-headed posts, even the vessels of these earlier Scandinavian voyagers must have borne quite a resemblance to their more perfect successors, the warships of the Viking era.

In an age when everybody was on the move, these early Scandinavian migrations were unexceptional; in a time when Christianity and western learning were hanging on 'by the skin of their teeth', pagan and barbarian conduct was not noteworthy. The reason our Viking era (770–1070) was the first time in history that the Danes, Norwegians and Swedes 'hit the headlines' and became known, indeed notorious, in the rest of Europe was not because they were doing anything fresh or unusual but because they kept on doing it with exceptional vigour after the rest had (comparatively speaking) stopped. The wails of horror and indignation the Vikings aroused, particularly from churchmen, were partly due to the extreme degree of their piracy and paganism but more to the fact that by then the rest of western Europe had (or liked to think it had) abandoned piracy and paganism in favour of more civilized and Christian ways. Then again, though Scandinavians were soon to prove themselves outstanding as merchants and traders, their ideas of commerce in these early days were limited to two; goods were transferred either willingly as a gift or unwillingly by theft and the Vikings' preference for the latter could not be expected to endear them to the mercantile world of their day.

Scandinavian unity

Enough has been said to indicate that the Scandinavian world had been continuing on a steady course of development many centuries before the Viking era. What are the characteristics common to that world that justify our speaking of it in general terms and as a unit?

The first of these is language; one of the factors making for Scandinavian identity (and thus facilitating joint enterprises by Danes, Norwegians and Swedes) was the general currency over the whole area of the Old Norse language, or, as it was more generally called, the 'Danish tongue'—*dönsk tunga, norræn tunga* or *Norræna*. Before the beginning of the Viking period, this primitive Nordic language had become differentiated from the German dialects spoken to the south of Scandinavia or in the Saxon region of England. The currency of *Norræna* in the Scandinavian homelands was already fairly wide, since it was spoken from the rivers Eider and Slie (the old time frontier of Denmark and boundary with Germanic lands) up to the North Cape, a distance as the raven flies of over 2,000 kilometres (1,300 miles). From east to west Scandinavia extended from the Åland islands to the North Sea coast—some 800 kilometres (500 miles). When the Vikings carried out their colonization of the British and other Atlantic isles and of Iceland and Greenland their language spread with them and was spoken over an immensely wider area.

Sometimes, as in Iceland, it remained the sole tongue of the inhabitants and survived down the centuries virtually unaltered. Sometimes (e.g. in Danelaw England) the old Norse tongue encountered a speech so near and sympathetic that a long term synthesis and a mutual enrichment were possible. At the other extreme the gulf between the Viking tongue and that of the country they invaded was too great for any degree of assimilation to take place, and in this instance (as in Ireland and Normandy) the Norsemen dropped their own language and adopted that of the natives. In these lands all that would survive of *Norræna* would be a few words in everyday use and a scatter of hybrid place-names.

Another characteristic common to Scandinavia from early times would seem to be a considerable uniformity of racial stock over the region as a whole. The study of physical anthropology indicates that by the later Bronze Age (say around 1000 BC) similar ancestral types were to be found all over the vast northern expanses, though some outside influences from the east and the south must of course have been at work; it is generally accepted that the bulk of the Danish population even today is racially the same as it was 3 to 4000 years ago.

It would also seem that by this time Norway, Sweden and Denmark (as they would later become) had developed a common indigenous culture and that what may reasonably be called a 'northern spirit' had already come into being in these northern lands. One of the popular misconceptions about the Vikings seems to be that they were a sort of *lusus naturae*, a freak of nature like a plague of locusts out of the unknown, people somehow cut off from the life of normal human communities and from any settled background. The evidence of archaeology and anthropology, however, quite clearly indicates that the prehistoric cultures of Scandinavia were more splendid, its population more homogeneous than in the lands to the south and west.

The Neolithic and Bronze Age cultures of Britain for example have left behind much less impressive artefacts than those of little Denmark; and compared with Scandinavian homogeneity the British population at the beginning of the Viking era was (and has to some extent remained) at best an uneasy amalgam of all the races that had invaded the islands during the previous 1000 years and at worst an irregular jigsaw of warring states.

In the British Isles the era of greatest progress had been the Iron Age when a large part of the islands had for better or for worse been pulled into

A collar of dancing men worked from the gold that began to flow north in the first four centuries AD. ►

the mainstream of Europe by two Iron Age peoples, each endowed with outstanding talents and each so much at variance with the other—the Celts and the Romans. On balance it was a misfortune to the Scandinavian peoples (as it was to the Germanic ones) that they did not undergo their period of subjection to the Pax Romana, and that the Celtic and Roman Iron Ages were for Scandinavia a time of relative enfeeblement and estrangement from the rest of Europe. This long period of isolation—it lasted at least from the third century BC to the fifth century AD—occurred when most of Europe was developing new political concepts and new life-styles; and it was to a large extent the reason why, at the beginning of the Viking era, the Scandinavian lands still lagged behind those which had been Romanized. For though the latter had temporarily lapsed into comparative barbarism they either still retained or soon reintroduced much of the legacy of the Roman Empire—not least the Christian religion. By 800, Charlemagne was the outstanding protagonist both of Christianity and of imperialism and between the subjects of his 'Holy Roman Empire' and those of king Godfred of Denmark there was now a great gulf fixed. In the northern countries inbred habits of thought and superstition, and rigid social customs had been coalescing for centuries undisturbed by outside influences. The Scandinavians instinctively distrusted Charlemagne's neo-Imperialism and Christianity alike. In fact they (and the Saxons too) could not rid themselves of the fear that Christianity and subservience to a foreign ruler might be one and the same thing!

The Scandinavian nations

We must now attempt to sort out and identify some of the tribes, nations and known locations of Scandinavia and take a look at the physical appearance of this vast territory as it was during the centuries leading up to the Viking era. The interest of Tacitus (c. AD 90) in the shape of northern ships has already been noted; he also makes reference to a number of tribes, the most powerful in the Scandinavian region being the Sviones, undoubtedly the Svear or Swedes of central Sweden.

As for the actual name Scandinavia, this is first referred to in writing by the elder Pliny who calls it 'Scadinavia, the largest of the islands beyond Jutland'. For the first surviving map of this remote part of Europe we have to wait until around AD 140. Its maker, the Graeco-Egyptian mathematician and geographer Claudius Ptolemy, also thought of Scandia (Skåne) as an island, and, quite correctly, as the largest and westernmost of the Scandian group. Ptolemy was not to know that Skåne is merely the tiny bracket on which (to be fanciful) the vast sitting-on-her-heels figure of Scandinavia rests her left knee. That he thought it an island is excusable since later writers refer to 'the great island Scanzia' and even the historian Adam of Bremen, writing in about 1075, thought of Skåne as 'nearly an island since it is

◄ *One of a number of helmets found with a formidable array of other armour in a 6th/7th-century cemetery at Vendel.*

surrounded by the sea on all sides except the frontier with Sweden, where there are deep forests and trackless mountains'. Students of Ptolemy's map will notice that he also gave too much prominence to the 'Saxon Isles'— what we should now call the North Frisian islands—and greatly over-emphasized the width of the Lim fjord in northern Jutland which caused him to place the 'Alokiai isles' (Thy, Mors and their neighbours) right out in the North Sea.

On the subject of tribes in the Scandinavian peninsula Ptolemy mentions the Goutoi and the Chaideinoi who can reasonably be identified with the inhabitants of Götaland in Sweden and Hedemark in Norway. After this there is an exceptionally long gap; it is four centuries before Scandinavia is again mentioned by the geographers or historians. The narrator this time is Jordanes, the historian of the Goths, who around 540 gave a geographical description in some detail of Britain and Sweden (Scanzia) from which the Goths under their king Berig migrated across the Baltic into Lithuania and thence to the shores of the Black Sea where they divided into Visigoths and Ostrogoths—an early 'Viking' movement to the east! Jordanes also gives some useful sixth-century information about the Svehans and Svetidi (Swedes), the Hallin of Halland, the Harothi of Hordaland, the Rugi of Rogaland and many other identifiable Scandinavian people. And it is he who, for the first time in history, mentions the Dani who between 200 and 500 had driven out the earlier occupants, the Eruli, and settled in Jutland and in the islands to the east of it. For the first recorded use of the actual word Denmark (Denemearc) we have to wait until the late ninth century and the historical writings of king Alfred the Great.

About the same time as Jordanes, a historian in Constantinople, Procopius, broke new ground by describing the peoples further north in Scandinavia, including a detailed and highly recognizable account of the habits, clothing and general economy of the Lapps. All these sources of information—and there may have been a number of others, now lost—indicate that the lands from which the Vikings were about to emerge were, though on the fringe of the civilized world, at least moderately well known to their more literate southern neighbours. By the end of the Viking period Adam of Bremen had acquired a good idea of the vastness of Sweden and Norway from his conversations with Svein Estridsson: 'The well-informed King of Denmark has told me that it takes a month or more to travel through Norway, and that one can hardly journey through Sweden in two'. This knowledge was not so widespread, detailed or accurate as to prevent contemporary historians and geographers from falling into frequent error; in an age of meagre communications it could scarcely be otherwise. But, on the other hand, it need not surprise us too much if, for example, the compiler of the Anglo-Saxon Chronicle is able to assert—even though writing 100 years later—that the raiders in the fateful year 789 came not only from Norway but from one particular and correctly named region of that country.

The main towns and regions associated with the Viking age in Scandinavia.

Around 890 England received first-hand information of Scandinavia and its trade routes from a shipman of northern Norway called Ohthere who visited king Alfred's court and dictated accounts of his voyages ranging from the White Sea to the Slie.

Social structure

Except in the far North, where the Lapps were still nomadic hunters, Scandinavia was now a settled agrarian society. That being so, the natural unit of human life was the family, or extended family, living in farmsteads. In some parts—the mountains and fjords of Norway for example—isolated farmsteads remained the basic topographical unit. In other parts, such as the Danish islands, farms would tend to be grouped together to form villages. How much these villages are identifiable with later parishes and how much they were themselves organized into larger administrative districts are still problems not entirely clarified, but it is thought that the villages of Denmark in Viking times were grouped into about 200 such districts, known as *herreds*.

Since *hær*, the first syllable of herred, means 'army' it is argued that the division of the country into these districts was connected with the levying of the population for purposes of war. It is likely that this system of herreds extended from Denmark into western Sweden and southern Norway; in Norway the districts were called *bygths* and in Sweden there were *hundares* which were based on organization for war and later were also linked with the parochial system.

The human element in the herred, bygth and hundare was the *thing*, the assembly of all free men of military age which met to give judgment and administer the law, this being handed down by word of mouth and from the memory of the older members. Above the individual herred, each with its thing, were the regional assemblies known as *Landthings*; in Denmark these were held at Lund (in Skåne), at Viborg (in Jutland) and at Ringsted on the island of Zealand; in central Sweden they were at Birka and Uppsala

All these were 'grass roots' institutions, democratically based and very different from the feudal system imposed from above which was now beginning to spread its tentacles over the Frankish and Germanic kingdoms to the south of Scandinavia. The tenure of land in the northern countries seems to have been purely allodial—that is to say each freeman owned his farm outright as the result of communal allotment or simply by right of occupation. This absence of allegiance in land tenure did not of course imply that society was completely egalitarian. In the first place, it was based on a large substructure of slavery; secondly, though all free men were nominally equal there were obviously at all times families who had had a run of luck in agriculture, or commerce, or war and by these means had accumulated riches and lands in advance of their fellows. Such families would probably intermarry, spreading their united estates and extending their authority over several herreds. From this ruling caste of *jarls* and *hersirs* sprang the petty kings of early Denmark, Norway and Sweden; and from these again by a process of elimination—especially during the tenth century—emerged the eventual ruling houses of the three nations. But even though it freely acknowledged class divisions, the society of Viking Scandinavia remained 'democratic' in that every free man had the right both to express his opinions and to better his lot. At the same time, the petty kings and even their more powerful successors were still answerable to the assembly of the free men for their authority and were first among equals rather than absolute rulers— 'mere top-dogs in . . . a hard-jawed pack', as Professor Jones puts it.

A picture of how the Scandinavians saw their own society and its origins has come down to us in the 'Song of Rig' (*Rigsthula*).

Rig, the father of mankind, comes to a cottage with a door ajar and a fire on the floor, where live a worn and ragged couple, Ai (great-grandfather) and Edda (great-grandmother), who give what food they can: 'unclean bread, lumpy and thick and full of husks', but with a bowl of soup and boiled veal. He gives them advice and gets into bed with them, stays for three days and nights, and nine months later Edda bears a son, Thrall, of whom it is said: 'the skin on his hands was wrinkled, his knuckles were swollen, his nails short, his face ugly, his fingers coarse, his back bent, and his heels long'; but he was a hard worker. Next there comes to the farm a girl called Thir (drudge): 'her legs were crooked, her feet dirty, her arms sunburnt, her nose pendulous'. She and Thrall produce children, a whole flock of them, a family of slaves.

Again Rig goes his ways. He comes to a hall with its door closed, he enters: there is a fire on the floor where sits Afi (grandfather) and Amma (grandmother), both at work. He, with hair covering his forehead and a well-cared-for beard, in a tight jacket, is skilfully making a loom; she, with a smock on her shoulders, a kerchief about her neck, and a linen cloth on her hair is turning the distaff and spinning the thread. Rig gives them advice and gets into bed with them and departs after three days. In nine months time Amma produces a child, a son called Karl (peasant or farmer), red and fresh and bright-eyed. He broke in oxen, made ploughs and tempered plough shares, built timbered houses and hay barns, and fashioned carts. Along comes a bride for him 'with the keys of the house, wearing a goat-skin jacket'. They have many children, and these become the peasant stock.

And again Rig is wandering. He comes to a hall facing south; its door decorated with rings, is open. He enters: there sat a couple on the floor strewn with rushes, their fingers busy—Fadir (father) and Modir (mother). The big farmer twisted a bowstring, bent an elmbow, made arrows; while the mistress looked at her arms, smoothed her clothes, tightened her sleeves. On her breast was a brooch, her shift was blue, her cap straight, her train long.

Rig gets into bed with them, stays three days and nights, and in nine months time Modir produces a son Jarl (earl) and wraps him in silks. Blond was his hair, his cheeks bright, his eyes piercing as a young serpent's. Jarl grows up, makes bows, rides horses, hunts with the hounds, is a fine swordsman and swimmer. He goes to war; he spurs his horse, strikes with his sword, raises warfare, stains the land with blood, slays his enemies. He then owns eighteen farms, and gives rich gifts of gold and horses to his friends. He marries Erna, the daughter of Hersi: beautiful, fair, and wise, her hands are slender. Of their children, the youngest son, Kon, is the outstanding one; it is he who will go a-viking and win kingdoms for himself.

Here then in poetic form are the constituent parts of northern society. First the slaves or thralls toiling at the most menial tasks, second the skilled farmers and artificers, free men and the backbone of the Viking people and of its armies, thirdly the class of 'big farmer', proficient in sport and war, from whom the fourth group, the jarls and hersirs sprang and consolidated their estates. Finally, from the marriage of Jarl and Erna the royal lineages are derived.

The Vikings themselves

Rígsthula also gives us a glimpse of how these different people looked, which may lead us to ask: 'What was the typical Viking's physical appearance? Were they all—as popular imagination and the advertising world would have us believe—bearded, blond (or red-haired) giants of at least 6′ 6″?'

From the scanty remains available of proven Viking date it would seem that the men were preponderantly of long-headed (dolichocephalic) Nordic type but the average height of both Danes and Icelanders seems to have been nearer 5′ 8″; the latter were of mixed Norwegian and Irish stock. It is thought that—as today—the Swedes may have averaged a little more in height—certainly their Arab contemporaries spoke of the Rus as 'tall as date-palms, . . . and all red-headed'.

It is sad that, with all their skill in wood and stone carving, the Vikings have not left us any portraits of themselves. The nearest thing to this genre are the heads from the Oseberg cart and the elk-horn stick handle from Sigtuna. The score for beards is, once again, three out of four—two being of shaggy type and one neatly trimmed. Moustaches are *de rigueur* and this is an adornment that was passed from the Vikings to their Norman descendants. The owners of hairless faces seem to have been liable to taunts from their fellows. A classic example is the Icelandic saga hero Njal: 'he was wealthy and handsome, but he had one peculiarity: he could not grow a beard'. Gunnar, the sub-hero of Njal's Saga, was the *beau ideal* in appearance and character: 'a tall powerful man, outstandingly skilful with arms . . . a handsome man, with fair skin and a straight nose slightly tilted at the tip. He had keen blue eyes, red cheeks, and a fine head of thick flaxen

Portraits of Vikings by Vikings are rare. In wood (above), in horn (below left) and in metal (below right) these three bear out Viking sagas and poems that habitually give the men moustaches, beards or both.

hair. He was extremely well-bred, fearless, generous and even-tempered, faithful to his friends but careful in his choice of them. He was prosperous.

Among the Indo-European peoples the description of individuals by their colouring has always been in fashion. 'Red' or 'black' or 'white' (not forgetting the intermediate mass of 'Browns') are among the most obvious nicknames. The Vikings were certainly not all blond beasts, though *Rigsthula's* distinction between black-skinned Thrall and fair-haired Jarl implies two groups in the population and perhaps even hints at the 'Nordic' myth of our own day.

In Egil's Saga the types are presented with no such invidiousness: we read how his grandfather Ulf had one son, handsome and lively, and another, dark and ill-favoured, and how the pattern repeats itself in the following generations. In the same way Halfdan the Black has three sons, two called Halfdan Black and White respectively and the third the famous Harald Fairhair.

The Irish made a useful distinction and may have hit on a general truth when they spoke of the Norwegian Vikings as white (*finn*) strangers and those from Denmark as black (*dubh*). The Welsh seem generally to have lumped together all ravaging Norsemen, pagans, devils and the like under the single epithet *duon*—black; though on one occasion we do get the distinction between a 'black troop' from Denmark and a 'white troop' from Lochlan (Norway)—so called, says Steenstrup, because of its *locs*, bays or fjords.

The origins of the three Scandinavian countries' names are not in any doubt and each to some extent incorporates a salient characteristic of the country itself. Thus DENMARK (*Danmark*) is the 'mark' or boundary state of the Danes; they have always held the chief land frontier of Scandinavia with the rest of Europe. SWEDEN (*Sverige*) is the kingdom (*rige*) of the Svear or Swedes: a state where from early times kingship was important. NORWAY (*Norge*) might seem on this analogy 'the northern kingdom'; but in fact it is what the English rightly (for once) call it, that is the 'north way', the long haul to the Arctic circle and beyond.

Some other Viking names are a matter of relative latitude and longitude. Thus the Danes called the Norwegians *Normannerne*—northmen, while to the Icelanders they were *Østmaend*—eastmen. Scandinavians in general called the Irish westmen, but to England they gave its proper name (or sometimes 'Anglia'), likewise Skotland, Bretland (the various sections of the Welsh), Irland, and, on the continent, Saksland, Flæmingeland and Valland for what became Normandy. The rather vague Norse name for the Muslim Empire was Serkland—the land either of silk or of Saracens. Russia was known either as 'Sweden the Great' or Garthariki —'The Kingdom of the Garthar or fortified towns', of which the chief was Mikligarth 'the great town' of Constantinople. To Byzantines and Arabs alike the Swedish Vikings in Russia from about 850 were 'Rus' a word probably derived from the Finnish name for Sweden: or else, from about 950 onwards, Βάραγγοί, Varangoi or Varangians, meaning 'men of the pledge' or confederates. The Arabs also called them *madjous*, 'heathen', and this aspect of the Vikings was likewise picked on by Latin writers with the words gentiles or *pagani*: in Latin, *Normanni*, *Dani* and *Pirati* were of course commonly used too. The French sometimes used *Vestfaldingi*—the men from Vestfold. The oddest word for the Vikings was the one used by the Germans: *Ascomanni*, Ashmen—perhaps because some of their ships were made of ash.

Finally we come to the word 'Viking' itself, which was used both by themselves and by others. It is a word about whose roots there is still doubt, and the reader may make his choice. If it is Old Norse it could be either (1) *vig* (battle) or (2) *vik*, common in place-names and meaning inlet, creek or bay (*Viken*, the Vik was what the Norsemen called the biggest inlet of all, the one between Scandinavia's 'thighs', which we now call Skagerrak), or (3) *vikja*, to move or turn away. A Viking can thus be one who does battle, one who lurks in inlets, especially the Inlet or one who moves (fast?) or turns away (from home?). But Viking could equally well come from (4) Old English *wic*, meaning camp, or (5) related Latin *vicus*, meaning trading-town as in Sleswic, Londonwic, Eoforwic, Quentowic and other famous trade centres of the period. Our Vikings can now be camp-folk or dwellers in towns for purposes of trade. One historian thinks that though Vik-ing did originally mean a northerner who visited vik-towns for trading purposes it later came to signify 'sea-robber' because these voyagers became better known for piracy than for trade. Since trade and piracy are closely related (one bargains with guile and money, the other with guile and weapons) the wheel has now come full circle!

Viking towns and trade

Towns and trading-stations are among the most remarkable phenomena of the Viking Age and in addition to those already mentioned we must now look briefly at some of the most important ones. But before we do so it may be useful to have some idea of the type of trade which called these places into existence. What during the Viking era were the goods which the northern lands required from the south and east and what were those which they had to give in exchange?

For those in the first category, incoming goods, our evidence is largely archaeological; it comes from things excavated at the trading centres themselves, from Viking habitation sites and (at least during pagan times) from graves. In the Viking context it is even more difficult than usual to distinguish between trade goods and loot.

First in the list of imports come silver and gold and jewels. For silver especially, the Scandinavians had an insatiable appetite since, apart from its

Glass and silver were luxuries the Vikings had to import. But trade with one wealthy port, Dorestad, soon gave way to pillaging. Repeatedly sacked, then badly flooded, the town sank into obscurity. Ruisdael's painting (below) shows only a few houses and a windmill there by the 17th century.

use as a metal, it was also the principal standard of exchange long before the first national Scandinavian coinages were minted from it in the late tenth century. Then there were the useful minerals, tin and copper, which together make bronze. There were quernstones, then pottery and glass, much of which was made in the Rhineland and imported either purely for its own sake or for the commodities (such as wine) which it contained. Lastly, there were certain things which by their nature leave little or no archaeological trace—salt and spices, woollen cloth, silks from the east.

The second category, northern commodities exported from the Viking lands, is a lengthy one. From prehistoric times Baltic amber had been the North's unique and prized contribution to the rest of the world, and no doubt some of the magical electric substance continued to be exported. Then there was soapstone from Norway and iron from Norway and Sweden either in bar form or as axes. There follows the long list of organic products of northern lands and seas—the skins, horns, hides and furs of many animals large and small; feathers and down from birds; morse ivory from the walrus or morse, whose hide (says Ohthere) was, like whale's hide, very good for ships' ropes; seal and whale oil; honey; horses; timber; and, above all, human beings as slaves.

As we have seen, slavery was an integral part of the northern world, as indeed it was of most contemporary societies; supply and demand were thus equally unaffected by any scruples. Thraldom was constantly recruited from criminals, debtors and other unfortunates, also by wars, Viking raids and deliberately organized slave-hunts among the Slavic tribes of Wendland.

In Roman times the Mediterranean world had welcomed and depended on a steady supply of Celtic and Germanic slaves—the girls nubile and the men strong and hardworking. Now the Viking merchants reopened the old trade routes and with great profit to themselves extended them to a whole new world of customers, the world of Islam, whose appetite for human flesh, especially female human flesh, was more voracious than ever Rome's had been.

Though many of the chief Viking towns had a mixed function—defensive, administrative and so on—a number seem to have existed specifically as *wics* with their distinctive layout of a single street, widening into the market-place, and with situations relatively undefended but usually so tucked away along tortuous tunnels as to be secure from surprise attacks.

In Sweden the important trading towns were Helgö, Birka and Sigtuna, all situated on or near the great lake Mälar. Of these, Sigtuna had three early Christian churches, but Birka was the largest; indeed during its short existence it was perhaps the most important trading town of the Viking world, with contacts over a very wide area. It was the first of the Viking towns to be excavated and is also one of the best documented towns, since it was visited about 830 and 850 by the Frankish missionary Anskar who was allowed by king Björn to preach Christianity there. Birka was governed by its own 'thing' with a headman who became a Christian and built a church on his property. Anskar tells us that Birka and Dorestad were in contact with each other, until the latter's disappearance in the mid-ninth century. The archaeological evidence, particularly that of coins, indicates that Birka also ceased to exist around 980.

In Norway the chief centre of trade between about 800 and 900 was Kaupang at the entrance to Oslo fjord. Ohthere called it Sciringesheal, where 'a large sea runs up into the country', a fair description of the Vik. The site of this town has been continuously excavated since 1956 and a large number of cremation burials yielded much western European pottery and metalwork, looted principally from the British Isles, but hardly any coins.

The journey from Kaupang to the very important trading town of Hedeby (also called Sliestorp) took our shipman Ohthere five days' sailing: 'Denmark [the west coast of Sweden was then Danish] lay to port, while to starboard for three days was the open sea; and after that there was a further two days sail, during which Jutland, south Jutland and many islands lay to starboard . . . during those days the islands belonging to Denmark lay to port.' So Ohthere sailed to '*aet haethum*', as he called it, through the Little Belt, hugging the coast the whole way, as was his practice.

Hedeby—Sliestorp is referred to in 804 but existed fifty years before then. Its position on the borders of Denmark and the Germanic lands made it both commercially and politically important. Its own semi-circular earthwork protected it on the landward side and enclosed an area of 60 acres; this also formed the eastern starting point of the Danevirke, the great earth rampart begun early in the ninth century by king Godfred to defend Denmark against attacks from the south. The Danevirke ran from Hedeby on the Slie across to Hollingsted on the river Trene, a navigable branch of the Eider, one of those 'tarbets' or 'portages' so dear to the Viking merchant and warrior, for it meant that, inside the protection of the Danevirke, merchandise and men could cross from the Baltic to the North Sea in a mere ten mile overland journey. Hedeby, like Birka, had extensive commercial contacts with the whole trading world, and enough has survived of the town for archaeologists to gain an accurate impression of how it looked. Like Birka again, Hedeby was one of the doors through which that indefatigable missionary Anskar strove to introduce Christianity into Scandinavia. After initial failures in the 820s he built a church at Hedeby in 832, though the fact that some years passed before its bell could be rung (it might frighten the other gods) indicates the ambivalent attitude of the Vikings toward the Christian religion. In fact, archaeological finds reveal that paganism and Christianity co-existed at Hedeby for another century at least and many Vikings who wished to trade with Christians would consider being marked with a cross a quite sufficient concession to make. As late as 950, the Arab Al-Tartushi reported: 'Except for a few who are Christians and have a

A man's name meaning 'army wolf' is inscribed on a stone at the side of the Hærvej, *the 'army road' running south through Jutland, across the Danevirke near Hedeby and into Germany.*

church there the people of the town worship Sirius,' and he added (though we need not assume he is referring to church singing): 'I have never heard more horrible singing than the Slesvigers—it is like a growl coming out of their throats, or like the barking of dogs, only much more beastly.'

Around the mid-eleventh century the town was decaying and was abandoned after attacks by Norwegians and Wends. It was succeeded by Slesvig, the modern town on the northern bank of the Slie fjord. This area of the old Danish kingdom is now part of Germany, but one of the finest collections of Viking and earlier Scandinavian archaeology to be found outside Scandinavia is housed at Gottorp Slot, in the suburbs of Slesvig.

Let us now make the sea-voyage from Hedeby to the other Baltic ports. 'Wulfstan [an English traveller reporting, like Ohthere, to king Alfred] said that he left Hedeby and came to Truso after seven days and nights and that the ship was under sail the whole voyage. Wendland [now Mecklenburg, Pomerania and East Prussia] lay to starboard, while to port were the Danish islands of Langeland, Lolland and Falster, also Skåne. After that Bornholm [Burgundarland] which has its own king, was seen to port and after that we had to port first Blekinge and Möre, then Åland and Gotland, all belonging to the Swedes. Wendland lay to starboard all the way—right up to the mouth of the river Vistula.' (A glance at a map suggests that, after Wulfstan's ship had passed Bornholm the wind must have backed east to cause this enormous tack up to Gotland and down to Danzig Bay—and explains why his voyage—a shorter one than Ohthere's from Kaupang— took two days longer.) Truso, the trading port they were seeking, was probably situated near present-day Elblag, where many Norse weapons and graves have been excavated.

Further up the Baltic's eastern shore were several other trading centres, but the most important one in this whole region was the island of Gotland. No port in particular, but rather the whole island seems to have been dedicated to trade over a period beginning in the early Iron Age and continuing right through to the Middle Ages and the era of the Hanseatic League.

Among many other archaeological finds, 100,000 coins, Arab, German and Anglo-Saxon, have been recovered from Gotland, which (since these are only a fraction of the total in circulation) suggests trade on a very considerable scale.

Moving back to the western Baltic, one other apparently Viking settlement must be named. It was situated in Wendland near the mouth of the Oder in the same sort of enclosed lagoon as Truso and other towns. Its name, according to Adam of Bremen, was Jumne (modern Wollin) and since archaeology has revealed a mixed Slav-Nordic population living there in the tenth and eleventh centuries it may have been the site of the Viking fortress of Jomsborg, founded by Harald Bluetooth, whose last wife was a Wend princess. Whether (on the strength of resemblance of name) Jumne was the home of the Jomsvikings, we do not know, but since their Jomsvikinga Saga is fiction rather than fact they themselves must remain 'legendary'.

Still further south and east, in what is now Russia, Poland and Romania, the main centres of Viking trade were situated on mightier rivers than the Vistula or Oder—the Dvina, ('the route to the Varangians') Dnieper, Volkhov, Volga and Don.

In the lands of the Franks, in north-west Europe, rivers played a different part in Viking operations. These had been enemy territories to Scandinavians ever since king Godfred in the early ninth century had resisted the encroachments of Charlemagne. It was therefore plunder and revenge, not trade, that drew the Viking raiders up rivers like the Weser, Ems, Ijssel, Rhine, Maas and Scheldt, and south as far as the Seine and Loire. The Carolingian fortress and mint-town of Dorestad, for example, situated on a branch of the Rhine, was reported to be the largest international market town in north-west Europe, but under the ineffectual successors of Charlemagne it was systematically pillaged by the Vikings from 834 onwards; coins from its mint were circulated and copied all over Scandinavia. Whether the Scandinavians would eventually have re-constituted it as one of their own trading centres, we cannot tell, since, not long afterwards, the great North Sea inundations of 864 altered the course of that part of the Rhine and left it stranded in a backwater—the 'Wijk by Dorestad' of Ruisdael's peaceful windmill scene. Further south on the Straits of Dover stood the Frankish market town and mint of Quentowic, which never recovered from its sack by Viking troops in 842.

Over in Britain the pattern was different. There is no doubt that the raiders of the early ninth century looked on the trading centres of Wessex and Mercia mainly as sources of loot and slaves—London, Southampton, Rochester and Canterbury all suffered in this way. But once the Vikings felt they had gained a stake in the land—as they did after the setting up of the Danelaw in 878—they began to take over towns like the 'Five Boroughs'—Leicester, Derby, Lincoln, Nottingham and Stamford—and convert them to their own use as centres for craftsmen and for local trade. York, as we have seen, had the status of an international trading centre. There were probably other marts in Viking England—perhaps Chester, and Torksey on the Trent, but the surviving evidence is so scanty it is hard to be certain. Likewise in Normandy, towns like Rouen which had previously been sacked by the Vikings later became their commercial centres.

In Ireland, where the population had not previously been town-dwellers it was necessary for the Vikings to form their own new settlements and harbours round the coast before they could carry on trading activities: Dublin, Cork, Limerick, Waterford and Wexford are the most important of these.

In concluding this brief survey of places in the Viking world we should remember that a very large number of farmsteads, villages and towns still existing in Scandinavia today were already in being in the later Viking period. In Iceland many of the farm sites mentioned in the sagas have remained inhabited till now, and this is no doubt the case with innumerable farm and village sites in the Viking home-lands as well as in the lands they colonized. Among the larger and more important places, Sigtuna, mentioned above, still exists as a Swedish town; so do Lund, Skara and Södertalje. In Denmark, modern towns with their roots in Viking times include Ribe, Aarhus, Viborg, Aalborg, Odense, Roskilde and Ringsted; and in Norway, Oslo, Bergen and Trondheim (then called Nidaros) were founded during the Viking period, albeit at the end of it. Copenhagen and Stockholm were not founded until the twelfth and thirteenth centuries respectively.

Early leaders

In most of this examination of the geography of northern lands and the general background of the Scandinavian peoples we have been on relatively safe ground. Places, after all, are fairly firmly anchored; though sometimes affected by large-scale natural phenomena like inundations or the rising and falling of the land, they (or their ruins) have a definite location. Troy town may have been covered up with weeds, and forgotten, but its site was still there waiting for Schliemann to rediscover it 2,000 years later.

But when we turn from geography to biography and from places to people, when we try to apply names and dates to individual persons and to elucidate the history of even the rulers and leaders during pre-Viking and early Viking times we are on less sure ground. Although the written source-material—chronicles, sagas and inscriptions—is there in abundance, modern critical examination has conditioned historians into rejecting most of it outright and accepting as historical fact only what can be checked against archaeological evidence.

However, the ordinary reader's best guide to this unknown region still remains the historian who dares to walk towards it with all his instincts alert and who is not afraid to use aesthetic considerations in arranging and interpreting the tiny signals he receives; or (to change the metaphor) takes good care as he sluices out the turbid waters of 'unhistorical sources' that the small but authentic offspring of Clio remains safely in the bath. Up to now the only such creative historian to attempt a portrayal of the Vikings' historical background is Professor Gwyn Jones. For the legends and traditions of the three northern peoples and their leaders one can only recommend with admiration the Introduction and relevant sections of chapters 1 and 2 of his *History of the Vikings*.

In this shorter work, lack of space—and poetic imagination—will confine our survey to those rulers of the emergent Viking countries whose

Imported pottery found with other foreign goods in merchants' ►
graves at Birka.

existence as historical figures is beyond reasonable doubt, even though their regnal years cannot always be accurately given.

Denmark remains legend-shrouded down to the 780s, the era when Charlemagne was subduing and evangelizing the heathen Saxon tribes living between his Frankish empire and the Danish border, also the era of the first wave of Viking attacks on England. By now a single ruling family seems to have established itself in Denmark, of which the head was king Sigfred.

Sigfred was succeeded in about 800 by Godfred who, in defence of Danish territory and profitable trade routes, is known to have retaliated vigorously against Charlemagne's expansionist activities—it was the beginning of a thousand year conflict between Danes and Germans. These trade routes defended by king Godfred ran east and west between the Baltic and the North Sea and north and south from Jutland down to the Elbe. It was at their point of intersection that the town of Hedeby and its associated system of defences, the Danevirke, were constructed; or anyway the earlier part of them, which the Frankish annals referred to in 808 as 'King Godfred's wall'.

In 810 Godfred made a successful expedition into Friesland, and, according to Charlemagne's biographer, was beginning to talk of bearding the emperor at Aachen, when he was murdered. Godfred was succeeded by his nephew Hemming who concluded a peace treaty between Denmark and the Holy Roman Empire in 811. This recognized the Eider as the Danish frontier—*Eidora Romani terminus imperii*; it is the earliest treaty in which any Scandinavian political unit is known to have participated.

If, from this time onwards, a strong unbroken line of kings had continued in Denmark this might well have altered the whole character and pattern of Danish Viking activity during the next two centuries. The language and treaty of diplomacy (as against mere force and expediency) used for the first time by king Godfred and king Hemming would have continued to be used by their successors. Hostilities between, for example, Denmark and Wessex would have been conducted not through the aggressive initiative of individual Viking bands but through diplomatic contact between ruler and ruler—and only after a declaration of war had been made.

But such diplomatic niceties can only be used when a country is united under a single government or ruler and after Hemming's death in 811 no such monarch was to be found in Denmark for another century and a quarter. Kings of a sort appear and disappear—Horik (the most celebrated), Harald Klak, Rorik, Halfdan, another Sigfred and Godfred, even a Swedish king Olaf and his successors Gnupa and Sigtrygg. Christian churches were built, Danes were baptized (and no doubt relapsed again) but, since there was as yet no native monastic foundation to 'keep the score' with its annals and chronicles, this period from 811–936 is one of obscure turmoil inside Denmark. It was an appropriate background for the tumultuous welter of Viking adventures in which her young men were engaging themselves

◄ *Silver, for ear-rings such as these from Torsta in Sweden, was much coveted by the Vikings.*

overseas. When the mists finally cleared around 936, the line of Swedish rulers has left the country and Gammel Gorm, king Gorm the Old, is revealed occupying the throne of a seemingly united and independent Denmark. From Gorm downwards the mighty line of Jelling kings and the later rulers of Denmark are a matter of agreed historical fact.

Until the second half of the ninth century the political history of Norway and its rulers shares the same obscurity as Denmark. It was, as we have seen, a country divided by its geography into a large number of self-governing districts, both great and small. The names of many of the larger units end in 'land' or 'mark' or 'rike' (kingdom). Each of these had its chieftains, some of them called 'kings' and, as in the legendary period of Denmark, strings of their names can be quoted—many on the entertaining but dubious authority of Snorri Sturluson, who alas! wrote his *Ynglinga Saga* three or four centuries later than the events it purports to describe. Olaf the Woodcutter, Halfdan Whiteleg, Eystein Fart and Gudrod are a few of these 'less than historical' kinglets. But with the last-named (who perhaps died about 840) we are at least approaching the realm of history, for Gudrod was reputed the father of Halfdan the Black, and Halfdan was the un-disputed parent of Harald Fairhair, the first who could claim to be king of a united Norway. Significantly it is with Halfdan the Black that Snorri begins the sagas, grouped under the title *Heimskringla*, of those whom he con-siders to be fully authenticated kings of Norway.

Still less is known about the early rulers of Sweden, where the dawn of historical certainty breaks even later than in the other two Scandinavian countries. The principal tribes of Sweden—Svear to the north and Götar to the south—were indeed known to historians by the second century AD and the continuing rivalry between these tribes and their 'kings' was the basic ingredient of Sweden's confused early history. These legendary rulers are many: the Old English poem *Beowulf* performs the same sort of service (or disservice) to our knowledge of them as the *Ynglinga Saga* does for their Norwegian contemporaries. Among those whose names emerge are Hygelac (*c.* 520), Ohthere (not to be confused with our shipman), Athils or Eadgils (17th in descent from the god Frey), Ivar, Harald Wartooth, Olaf and Onundr, the last-named encountered by the missionary Anskar and so datable to about 840.

The ninth century is the period of Sweden's great eastern movement but, as in Denmark, Viking activities abroad do not necessarily throw any light on rulers at home. Even in the tenth century, when a fairly clear picture is available elsewhere in Scandinavia, events in Sweden are still obscure. A king named Eirik the Victorious is reputed to have defeated the Danes around 980, but it is not until the arrival on the scene of king Olaf Skötkonung about the year 1000 that an undisputed *Rex Sveorum et Gothorum* can be said to have emerged. This is the time too when the Christian religion begins to filter into Sweden.

The success of the Viking movement depended on its ships. The Gokstad ship (above) and a sketch on a piece of wood found at Bergen demonstrate some of the unique characteristics of Viking ship-building: the planking combined maximum strength with minimum weight; the mast was stepped to allow even distribution of stress but ease in raising and lowering it; and the rudder, while projecting below the keel as 'centre board', could be quickly lifted clear when the boat was beached.

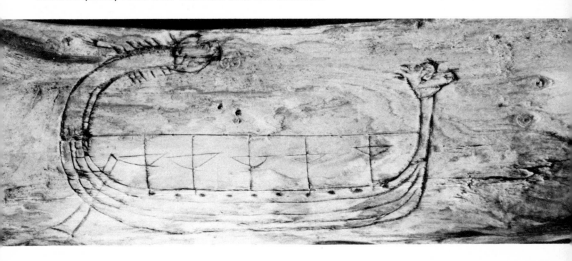

According to *Heimskringla*, Olaf was succeeded in 1022 by his son Onund Jacob, who was thus a contemporary of Knut the Great, whom he met in battle at the Holy River. With the death in 1060 of Onund Jacob's brother Emund, this first authenticated line of Swedish kings dies out. A period of obscurity and civil war follows until the twelfth century; indeed it was not till then that Sweden was fully converted to Christianity.

Causes of the Viking movement

In their broadest sense the origins of the Viking movement are implicit in everything that has been said so far about the Vikings' geographical and historical background. The desire for fame and glory, for land and material possessions, and for the wealth to acquire them springs eternal in the human breast. Its power of motivation is neither stronger nor weaker in the ninth century AD than it would be in the nineteenth, or for that matter had been in the ninth century BC, and besides human nature, we have observed other factors which over a long period had also remained virtually constant.

One thing seems certain; unlike the great folk-migrations which had taken place at the end of the Roman Empire, the Viking movement was in the main not the result of external pressures by other nations on the people of Scandinavia. Nor must causes be confused with means: better ships and improved methods of navigation were absolutely fundamental to the success of Viking activity, whether in raiding, trading or colonizing, but they were one of its instruments, not its cause.

The assignment of causes is itself something which tends to follow historical fashion. In the heyday of the political historian—say around 1900—the most favoured explanations of the Viking movement were, as might be expected, political ones. Social and economic influences like the desire for riches or a hunger for land were, for example, less admissible as explanations for the Norwegian emigrations to Iceland and Britain than the ruthless political unification of Norway by Harald Fairhair (but this theory has since come partly unstuck because of a discrepancy in dates between cause and effect!).

For the last half century, on the other hand, an increasing number of historical writers have ascribed more weight to economic causes than to political ones. These historians would attribute the movement east of Swedish Vikings to the newly arisen opportunities for trade with the Muslim Empire, and to the initiative of the Rus in creating an entrepôt for merchandise between the Near East and north-west Europe. Some economic historians would in fact go further and affirm that this whole 'shining period' in northern history was the result of Scandinavian control of the main transit territory for east-west trade.

A third branch of historical study has been making rapid growth over the past 30 years or so. This is social history, which has stimulated the interest of rather a wider public than political or economic history has ever done. Social history studies have been much enhanced by new types of museum, specializing in European ethnology, which have collected and displayed an enormous range of material illustrating the cultures of their own regions or countries. Beginning in Sweden in 1873 these social history or folk museums have now spread all over N.W. Europe and, closely linked with them, there has been a proliferation of institutions and societies devoted to local history, social history, folk-life, archives, place-name studies, dialect studies and so on. Social historians, both amateur and professional, tend to look at the Viking phenomenon in terms of the above range of subjects. They find its deepest and most lasting significance in the long-term contributions which the Vikings made to the social development, the 'folk-life' of the countries they settled in, above all Britain, Iceland and Normandy. As for the causes of the movement they will look for these too in the fields of ethnography and social history: causes like the length of the northern winters, the social and sexual habits of the Scandinavians, or the insufficiency of their agriculture.

The ways in which these three kinds of historians—political, economic and social—examine the causes of the Viking movement are to some extent paralleled within the movement itself. Though all the three countries concerned had common aims and characteristics each also had distinctive qualities, tendencies and needs, giving it a role in the Viking drama different from those played by the other two. Thus the Vikings from eastward-facing Sweden and Gotland were pulled south and east by trade, while for Norway's land-starved farmers the slogan was 'go west, young man'! Denmark, the hub of the Scandinavian world, shared the other two countries' concerns with trade and emigration but, in addition, its kings early developed that desire (and ability) to dominate their neighbours which culminated in the eleventh-century empire of Knut the Great.

Desire for trade (and piracy), for land, and for political domination are three of the movement's causes whose validity is generally accepted as being beyond question.

Chapter III **Early Raids**

Wessex

From the 750s to the 790s the little Anglian and Saxon kingdoms which
made up England came increasingly under the dominance of king Offa of
Mercia, who styled himself 'King of all the English'; he was, perhaps, the
only ruler at this period in western Europe to be compared with Charlemagne, with whom he corresponded. Under the year 789, the Anglo-Saxon
Chronicle, having recorded the marriage of one of Offa's daughters with
Beorhtric, the rather obscure king of Wessex, continues: 'And in his days
came first three ships of Norwegians from Hordaland: and then the reeve
rode thither and tried to compel them to go to the royal manor, for he did
not know what they were: and they slew him. These were the first ships of the
Danes to come to England.' This typically curt account in the Chronicle can
be filled out by other early authorities: the place on the coast where the
Viking ships landed was Portland in Dorset, the name of the luckless reeve
was Beaduheard, and the royal manor from which he rode out to investigate
these foreign merchants was Dorchester, ten miles inland. The reeve had no
grounds for suspecting the strangers to be anything other than merchants
because, whatever England's internal dissensions, piracy on her coasts was
evidently not an expected hazard at this time. To the statement 'these were
the first ships of the Danes' the Latin version of the Chronicle adds: 'because
never before these had any others come, ever since the Angles first entered
Britain.' This rather surprising remark is echoed in the often-quoted lament
of the York-born scholar Alcuin four years later: 'It is nearly 350 years that
we and our forefathers have inhabited this most lovely land and never before
has such a terror appeared in Britain as we have now suffered from a pagan
race: nor was it thought that such an inroad from the sea could be made.'
Alcuin seems to have forgotten that his own Anglian ancestors in the 440s
had achieved a precisely similar invasion across the North Sea.

It is obvious from the 789 Chronicle passage that the Anglo-Saxons were confused on two points—and it was a confusion that persisted right through the Viking era. Firstly, they were never quite sure of the difference between a Dane and a Norwegian ('Northman') and tended to use both terms interchangeably; we can now be fairly certain that all the early raiders were in fact Norwegians and that in Iceland, in the islands and in the Celtic parts of Britain outside the field of English history they continued to be Norwegians; in the English kingdom and on the Continent from the 830s onwards they were predominantly Danes.

Secondly, with small bands of Northmen, say up to two ships and two or three dozen men, it can never have been easy for the English to decide whether peaceful trade was intended, or murder with robbery; and to avoid Beaduheard's fate it was a decision that had to be made both correctly and promptly! When greater numbers of ships and men were involved there could of course be little doubt as to the visitors' malevolent intentions. Even allowing for merchants travelling in convoy, a force of forty or fifty upwards could only mean a raid or, as the English called it, a 'here', referred to in the case of a really large host of invaders as a 'micel here'—a big raid. The choice of word is significant: it would be more normal to call a force of foreign invaders 'an army', or 'an enemy army' rather than a raid. But, like that of freebooters in all ages, the Vikings' impact, at least in these early years, was not the kind normally exerted by a settled society on its neighbours—no involvement at national level, therefore no machinery or diplomacy and no formal declaration of war. There may have been odd occasions when what looks like large-scale piracy turns out on examination to be an act of policy by one or other of the Scandinavian rulers. Professor Jones cites the sack of Hammaburg (the nucleus of modern Hamburg) by the Danes in 845 as an example of a royal, that is national, undertaking rather than piracy—not that the suffering inhabitants would appreciate the difference. But in England such examples are hardly to be found before the joint invasions of the kings of Norway and Denmark around the year 1000.

To a society which feels it has just moved into a more civilized way of conducting affairs, privateering is in itself particularly detestable, but the reputation that has stuck with the Vikings down the centuries was gained during their pioneer raids on Britain, and for a different reason. At this epoch their objective was not land—that came afterwards—but loot, and in particular silver, much prized in Scandinavia and not produced there. The Northmen very quickly learned that the richest storehouses of this portable wealth, churches and monasteries, were also the least well defended—the chief defence of a church, its holiness, and of a monastery, its isolation, being as nothing to these sea-borne pagans. Spiritual resources apart, the cleric had, however, one highly potent, albeit delayed-action weapon at his disposal—his literacy. If he could defend himself but feebly against axe and halberd, on parchment he could deplore in the strongest of language; and

The likelihood of loot drew the Viking raiders' attention to the churches of western Europe. One of the earliest attacks on England plundered the monastery of Lindisfarne, temptingly sited on an island off the North Sea coast (above). Next in line for attack were the Atlantic islands north of Britain, and then Ireland. This little saint (left) was carried back from Ireland to Norway.

though his outcry availed him nothing at the moment of terror, penned by his surviving brother into the monastic chronicle it has reviled and denounced the Vikings to all succeeding ages.

Northumbria

Let us now turn from Saxon Wessex to Anglian Northumbria and from the Anglo-Saxon Chronicle (whose chief concern was the political fortunes of Wessex) to a northern monastic chronicler, Symeon of Durham. Although he was actually writing around the year 1100, the earlier parts of Symeon's narrative were undoubtedly copied from an author who was recording events soon after their occurrence. Following a detailed description of Lindisfarne Island, with its 'noble monastery' and memories of St. Cuthbert, the chronicle continues: '*793*. In this same year the Pagans from the northern part of the world came like stinging hornets to Britain with their sea-going force: and running hither and thither like ravening wolves, plundering, devouring and slaughtering not only beasts of burden, sheep and cattle but also even priests and deacons and groups of monks and nuns they came to Lindisfarne Church. With lamentable pillage they lay waste everything in sight—trampling the holy relics and defiling them under foot, overthrowing the altars and seizing the treasure of the holy Church.

'Some of the monks they kill outright, others they overpower and carry away with them. A great many they taunt and abuse and fling out naked; others they drown in the sea. Then they depart, bragging about their plunder and their wicked deeds.

'In 794 the above-mentioned Pagans laid waste Jarrow, the port and monastery, situated on the estuary of the river Don (a tributary of the Tyne). But this time St. Cuthbert did not allow them to get away unscathed. Indeed, their leader was slain by the English, and soon afterwards a storm smashed up their ships. Most of the raiders were swallowed by the sea and as for the few who regained the shore, they were speedily and mercilessly put to death. Which served them right!—since, up to now they had done such grievous harm to others without suffering any themselves.'

The narrative of these two raids is clearly based on eye-witness accounts—perhaps of those lucky ones who, though 'taunted, abused and flung out naked', nevertheless survived to tell the tale; possibly it was the abbot Uigbald himself, who ruled the monastery from 760–803. Indisputably, these pioneer Vikings appear at their savage and destructive worst; but, senseless brutalities apart, we do learn from their accounts two of the practical objectives of a Viking raid—treasure and slaves. Unchallenged though they may have been in their Lindisfarne raid of 793, failure of their Jarrow expedition in 794 must have had the effect of dispelling from an early date any legend of Viking invincibility—for the Norsemen themselves as well as their victims. The sharp lesson taught them on England's north-east coast may well be one explanation for the country's 40-year period of freedom from Viking raids between 794 and 835.

Celtic Britain

However, the rest of Britain did not remain unscathed. Raids by Norwegians on the Orkneys, Shetlands, Hebrides, Isle of Man, Wales and above all on Ireland began (with a raid on the church on Lambey near Dublin) in 795 and continued throughout the first half of the ninth century. Hardly a year passes without the Annals of Ulster reporting plunder and destruction and 'the devastation of the Kingdom by gentiles'. In 820 the annalist records: 'The sea poured torrents of foreigners over Erin so that no harbour or landing place, stronghold or fort was without waves of Northmen and pirates.' Most likely the same events were occurring on the coasts of Wales, Scotland and the Isle of Man but lacked a regular chronicler to record them. In 836 a Norse fleet entered the river Liffey and established a permanent settlement on the 'Black Pool' (*Dubhlinn*) where a small monastery already existed.

With the arrival shortly before 840 in Ireland of the Norse leader Thorgils (or Thorgisl, or Turgeis), the attacks came to resemble not so much indiscriminate piracy as a deliberate Norwegian attempt to occupy the island. Thorgils is remembered by Norwegian as well as by Irish traditions as the first high king of Erin and first overlord of Dublin; a town which at this time acquired a temple dedicated to Thor, the Dubliners themselves being nicknamed 'Thor's people'. Up to this time the Irish had not been town or village dwellers, but now, besides Dublin, a string of other fortified harbours—Limerick, Wexford, Waterford, Cork and others—came into being. Unlike some of the other trading centres of the Viking world all these have remained inhabited towns, thus covering up the traces of the original Viking settlements. Thorgils was captured and drowned in 845 and from this time the Irish began to stage a comeback against their Norse oppressors. Help came from an unexpected quarter with the arrival in 849 of a Danish Viking fleet (via England) under the chieftain Orm. For the next few years the Irish were able to enjoy the pleasing spectacle of dog eating dog as the 'black strangers' (Danes) slaughtered the 'white strangers' (Norwegians) and despoiled them of their booty. 'And so God deprived them of what they had taken from churches, from altars, and from the Saints of Erin.' In 852 the tables were nearly turned in a fierce sea battle at Carlingford, but Orm (any port in a storm!) called on the protection of St. Patrick and gained a decisive victory. After which the Danes—always willing to propitiate any power which had proved itself effective—dedicated back to the Saint a chestful of the same gold and silver of which their fellow Vikings had so recently deprived him. 'They have at least a kind of piety' was the Irish chronicler's too-hopeful comment. Piety or no, this propitiatory act availed

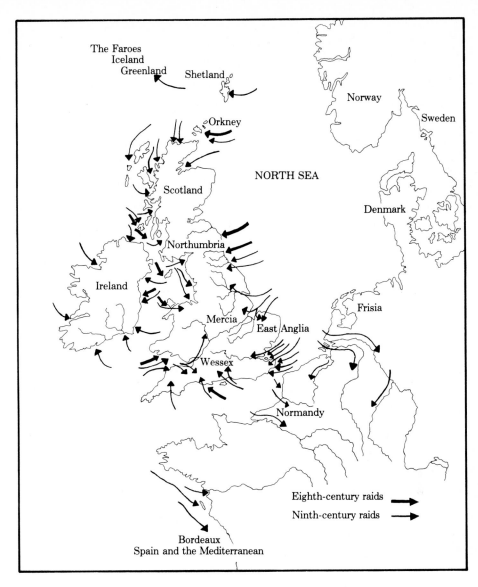

Viking raids on western Europe in the 8th and 9th centuries.

the Danes nothing when, next year, Olaf (perhaps Olaf the White of Norse tradition) arrived with a large fleet in the Liffey and speedily re-established the Norwegian upper hand in Ireland and a period of influence which lasted under Olaf and his brother Ivar and their successors until the beginning of the tenth century, and to a lesser degree until the Battle of Clontarf (1014) which ended Scandinavian rule in Ireland.

After relinquishing Erin to the superior Norwegian forces, Orm and his Danish Vikings seem to have turned their attention to other parts of the Irish sea. The Isle of Man was pillaged by the 'black strangers' in 853 and two years later the Annals of Ulster report that in an attack on North Wales Orm was killed by Rhodri Mawr, the king of that region. The Danish Vikings who raided Gower on the south Wales coast and were expelled from there in 860 were perhaps the last remnant of this band of raiders or would-be-settlers. For, following the general pattern of the Viking movement in western Europe, raiding was giving place to settlement from the mid-ninth century onwards. The re-establishment at this same time of Norse power in Ireland meant that the colonization of the other coasts of the Irish sea was also predominantly Norwegian in nature. This was the period of Norse occupation of the Isle of Man and of the Norwegian colonization of north-west England—from the Wirral northward—and of south-west Scotland. Neither in Danish nor Norwegian areas of settlement is archaeological evidence plentiful, perhaps because from early on many of the Vikings buried their dead in Christian graveyards and conformed (though still pagans themselves) with Christian burial practices; dispensing, that is, with the weapons, ornaments and grave goods by which they would otherwise have been readily distinguished from the Anglo-Saxons.

The evidence of place-names might reasonably be expected to fill some of the gaps left by archaeology, but in Ireland, Scotland, and the Isle of Man it largely fails to do so, principally because the difference between the Celtic native tongues and the speech of the invaders was generally too great to permit assimilation to take place at all extensively. There are of course towns in Ireland—Wicklow, Wexford, Waterford, Cork and others—with names that are clearly not of Celtic origin and some other places in Ireland and Man with recognizably Scandinavian names: Leixlip 'the salmon leap' is a graphic example. The name Ireland itself is Scandinavian as is the 'ster' (*stadr*) termination of three of its provinces. But in England, by contrast, and especially in the Anglian parts of the country the nearness of the languages involved and, in particular, the similarity between Anglian and Viking personal names made for an easy acceptance of the Scandinavian element in English place-names. In Normandy, on the other hand there was only a moderate degree of assimilation. The exception in Celtic Britain is that part of south-west Wales (Dyfed) that has always retained its separateness from the rest of the principality. Here, in 'Little England beyond Wales', the coast line from Fishguard round to Tenby is ringed with names of Scandinavian origin, and the hinterland is sprinkled with them also. The great fjord, Britain's finest natural harbour, was known to Dane and Norwegian alike as Midfjord Havn: along its shores many a ninth- or tenth-century Viking has left his name on the map of today.

England and the Continent

As we have seen, Danish Vikings began their activities round the Irish Sea from 849. On the English Channel and the southern coasts of the North Sea they had begun to make their presence felt some fifteen years earlier. Under the year 835 the Anglo-Saxon Chronicle makes the brief report: 'in this year the heathen devastated Sheppey.' It is a measure of the Chronicle's pre-occupation with the affairs of Wessex that, despite the known Viking activity around the Irish sea for the previous fifty years, the words 'pirates' and 'heathen' had never been mentioned! For the next eighty years scarcely one was to pass without some reference to their deeds either in Britain or on the Continent. During this period, when the other English kingdoms were being swept off the map by the invaders, Wessex and its able rulers fulfilled their destiny of uniting England as a nation. And the annals of Wessex, the Chronicle, from being a mere calendar of local happenings became the record of national events—a continuous annal such as no other nation of western Europe possessed. For sixty years indeed its almost exclusive concern is with the struggle of England and her neighbours against the Scandinavians: a blow by blow account unsurpassed by any other contemporary source, though matched in some respects for the period 830–882 by the French *Annales de St. Bertin*.

The mutual enmity and outright warfare between Danes and Norwegians which persisted in Ireland is not found further east. In their attacks on Friesland—especially the trading centre of Dorestad—Kent, Cornwall and the coastline and estuaries of northern France, the two Viking streams were joined together so that in any particular raid it would be difficult to distinguish the relative share of Danes and Norwegians. True, certain zones of Viking activity in western Europe seem to have remained exclusively Norwegian—the Hebrides, Iceland, Greenland, Orkneys, Shetlands and north-west England; but the 'here' which ravaged England, Frisia and France during the ninth century seems likely to have been recruited from all parts of Norway and Denmark, perhaps with a scattering from Sweden as well. We must remember that this is also the time when this third Scandinavian nation was beginning its own expeditions east and south along the rivers, lakes and inland seas of Russia.

Unlike the armies of the tenth and eleventh centuries, which were national and relatively large, these ninth-century hosts or 'heres' of mixed origin were probably quite small and never more than a thousand strong. Contemporary sources seldom refer to the numbers of men involved in raids or battles, but they do often make an effort at estimating how many ships took part. Ships are easier to count than men, and a small number of ships easier to count than a large one. Ten, twenty, thirty are likely to be enumerated with reasonable accuracy. Larger numbers—say over forty—may well lead to guess-work and guess-work to exaggeration. Thus, when the Anglo-Saxon Chronicle speaks of five ships or even twenty-five, the numbers are probably more to be trusted than when it tells of 250. Human nature (especially when explaining away a defeat) is very apt to add a nought!

The 835 raid on Sheppey was followed in the next eighteen years by a succession of others round the coast of England from Cornwall up to Lincolnshire. Though irritating and harmful, these were in the nature of sudden piratical raids and not yet on the scale which would later endanger the country itself. They were, however, part of a more general scheme of Viking operations directed against trading centres on both sides of the channel—London, Southampton, Rochester and Canterbury on the English side, Dorestad (on one of the mouths of the Rhine), Quentowic (near Etaples), Rouen, Bordeaux and Nantes on the Continent. On their side the Anglo-Saxon forces did sometimes gain the victory, but on the other side of the channel the Vikings seem to have consistently 'had possession of the place of slaughter'; indeed Dorestad and Quentowic, from having been important trading and mint towns, vanish altogether from history about this time. The Vikings made their cross-channel strategy much easier for themselves by acquiring a number of beach-heads well situated for attacks against either side of the Channel and of the kind on which they always felt themselves most secure, that is peninsulas or islands. Three of these—there were probably more—were: Noirmoutier in the mouth of the Loire, occupied in 849, Thanet, where, in 850, 'the heathen for the first time remained over the winter' and Sheppey at the mouth of the Thames, occupied in 855. With the acquisition of these permanent bases, going a-Viking was becoming, for the first time, not just a seasonal venture but an all the year round occupation. The long, hazardous, energy-consuming journeys back to the Vik or the Lim fjord were eliminated; instead women and other comforts of home were brought from Scandinavia. The bands of part-time pirates were on the way to becoming a regular professional army, whose objective was no longer just the raiding and looting of individual towns but the invasion and subjugation of the whole countryside.

The Scandinavians' progress towards this larger objective was very rapid indeed especially among the divided kingdoms of England. Of these, Deira, the southern part of Northumbria, fell between 855 and 867 and Bernicia its northern part by 875; East Anglia collapsed in 870 and Mercia, including London, between 869 and 874. Only Wessex weathered the storm, aided in this by the succession of king Aethelbert in 860 to a unified block of territory comprising Wessex, Sussex, Surrey, Kent and Essex. Although unable to prevent the sack of Winchester, he managed to defeat the pirate host in that year and in the years up to his death in 865, thus deflecting them for a time to weaker parts of the country. But in 865 'came a great heathen host to England and took winter quarters in East Anglia, and they were provided there with horses.' This army, mobile as never before, was under the command of a number of leaders whose names will recur during the next decade: Guthrum from Denmark and three brothers, Ivar the Boneless, Ubbe and Halfdan, sons of the Ragnar who had been ravaging Flanders and France since the 830s, and one who was nicknamed for the raven flag, the 'banner of destiny' (*Lodbrog*) under which he and his family sailed.

Until 874, when it started to split up, this standing army operated as a formidable single unit; and as Wessex became the last stronghold of Saxon independence so it had to withstand the main force of the Viking attack. The British Isles seemed on the point of becoming an extension of Scandinavia. But in 870 a notable event occurred: Aethelwulf's youngest son Alfred succeeded his three short-lived brothers on the throne of Wessex. Before the turn of the century Alfred's comparatively long reign and, above all, his personal genius, would have reversed what must have seemed at his accession a more probable tide of events.

Up to 878 the issue remained uncertain. In Alfred's first year as king he survived 'nine general engagements besides innumerable forays' and during the next six years successfully resisted two major attacks on Wessex by Guthrum. In these early years of Alfred's reign it was the collapse of the other English kingdoms (referred to above) and the opportunities this held out to the land-hungry Northmen that more than anything contributed to the salvation of Wessex; this and the nature of the Viking leadership. A national army of invaders serving the political ends of a foreign sovereign is not permitted to split itself up and enjoy the fruits of conquest until that conquest has been fully secured. Not so with the 'here'. It may have been a very large raid, but in essence a raid it remained; so that, when Halfdan's troops in 874–5, or other Danes two years later, felt the urge to share out the conquered territories of Northumbria and Mercia and settle down on them, there was no higher power to say them nay. Moreover, Ireland and Wales were still (from Alfred's point of view) useful diversions. Halfdan and his brother Ubbe may have spent much of 877 attacking Ivar of Dublin ('because Ivar had invaded Northumbria') and Ubbe wintered that year with his 23 ships and their Raven banner in Milford Haven—presumably at Hubberston—far from the West Saxon theatre of operations. In the spring of 878 he sailed thence to a crushing defeat and death at the mouth of the Taw in Devonshire; 'and there the banner which they call the Raven was captured'.

878 began, however, with Alfred's fortunes at their lowest ebb; at this period the 27-year old king had to bear great tribulations and lead a life of considerable personal discomfort. That winter Guthrum and his 'here' attempted their first actual partition of Wessex territory. No account by any later writer can be more graphic than that of the Anglo-Saxon Chronicle: 'In this year the host went secretly in midwinter after Twelfth Night [the 6th of January] to Chippenham and rode over Wessex and occupied it, and drove a great part of the inhabitants oversea, and of the rest the greater part they reduced to submission, except Alfred the King and he, with a small

company, moved under difficulties through woods and into inaccessible places in the marshes. And the Easter after, King Alfred with a small company built a fortification at Athelney, and from that fortification, with the men of that part of Somerset nearest to it, he continued fighting against the host. . . .'

For the year 878, like the years 937 and 1066, was to be one of the turning points in the early history of England, and the tide of events, when it did change, was miraculously rapid—some chroniclers recorded it as an actual miracle in which St. Cuthbert appeared to Alfred. Seven weeks and a day after Easter the king set up a rallying point for the West Saxons at Ecgbrihtesstane (Brixton) on the Wiltshire border. 'To their beloved leader, with hearts rejoicing, came all the inhabitants of Somerset, Wiltshire and Hampshire.' Three days later, at Edington just north of Salisbury Plain, this army of Wessex faced the 'immense phalanx of pagans' and inflicted a decisive defeat on them. After a fortnight's siege the Danes inside the royal vill of Chippenham surrendered. Guthrum submitted to baptism (his Christian name was Athelstan) at Alfred's hands, and thirty followers with him. The Danes had been clearly shown that in this part of England at least they had no chance of settlement and that the native levies under their young king were a force to be reckoned with.

The Peace of Wedmore which followed was a realistic treaty; it secured (at the expense of the Anglian part) the Saxon region of England. And to those of the Scandinavian host who wished to settle—'to plough the land and make a living for themselves'—it gave for the first time the opportunity to do so under at least a show of legality: under, indeed, their own Dane Law. It gave them a broad mass of territory extending diagonally across the waist of the island, with a long North Sea coastline facilitating settlement from Denmark, and a shorter Irish Sea one giving free access to the Norwegian settlements in Ireland. At least as far as Britain was concerned the Viking period of raiding, pillaging and living off the land was nearing its end, and an era of agricultural settlement was beginning. This is the point to remind ourselves that these were also the years when the fertile parts of Iceland—empty except for a scatter of Irish monks—were being partitioned and settled in a mainly law-abiding and orderly fashion by Vikings from Norway.

For those who still relished the Viking way of life, those whose temperament was only suited to military life, there was no lack of fresh territories to victimize on the Continent. But in England it was now possible for the first time to make a distinction between those Scandinavians who had become settlers and those who remained pirates. Under the year 879 the Anglo-Saxon Chronicle records Viking affairs in two sections: first the ex-army pioneers in the East Anglian part of the Danelaw 'who divided up their land and occupied it as settlers'; and second the band of unregenerate pirates, quartered at Fulham on the Thames, for whom the sword-into-

Prime instrument of the Viking's raids, his ship. ▶

ploughshare movement of their fellows held as yet no attractions and who, rather than abandon their piratical way of life, preferred to quit the island of Britain and carry on their raiding activities in France. But now it was raiding with a difference. The Northmen on the continent in the late ninth century were no longer scattered bands of independent seasonal pirates but members of a united and professional army, keeping the field year in year out, summer and winter. This army was their home, a settled community with its household of warriors, women and children, thralls and captives, all subsisting as a parasitic growth on the host country. 'All its operations were determined solely with the view to the upkeep of the army and as an outcome of its desire to plunder.'

For the next decade—and no doubt with some satisfaction at England's own respite—the Anglo-Saxon Chronicle relates in detail the sufferings of the Bretons and Franks, including their year-long siege of Paris in 885–6, with Hastein in command. The Vikings had been on the Somme and the Seine for the past forty years, and Paris had already been attacked by them in 845, 856 and 861.

During the ninth century they had also raided and invaded further north, in what is now Belgium, and were active on the Scheldt and the Maas around Namur and Liège where they had a camp called Ascloha (Hasloo); and, in 882, on the Rhine and the Moselle.

During this decade 881–91 the only untoward events mentioned in England were two naval encounters and an unsuccessful Viking attack on Rochester. But king Alfred was not yet allowed to finish his reign in peace. In a last assault on Wessex, in 892, Hastein, with his army from France, was joined by warriors from their new farms in the Danelaw, and because of this help it took Alfred four years to contain the invading army. But in the comparatively peaceful years between 879 and 892 the king had done much to improve England's defences: on land by a system of strongpoints and at sea by the building of a fleet of ships—the first English navy. But, most important of all, as the Chronicle tells us, 'the King had divided his levies into two sections, so that there was always half at home and half on active service, with the exception of those men whose duty it was to man the fortresses.' In 886 Alfred occupied London, afterwards entrusting it to Ethelred, a Mercian leader who later became his son-in-law and rendered faithful service for many years to Wessex. Much ingenuity was used during the war of 892–6 to frustrate the Danes and keep them on the move. When they tried to settle in the deserted Roman town of Chester the king applied scorched earth tactics to the country round and forced them to move from the Wirral into Wales; from Wales they made the long trek across to Essex eventually pulling their ships up the Thames and then (avoiding London) up the Lea. Alfred let the Danes go to the trouble of building a fort, twenty miles above London, then forced them to abandon both fort and ships by blocking the river. Nothing was wasted: 'all the ships they could not take away they broke up, and those that were serviceable they brought to London.'

But the king did not rely only on captured vessels; he was designing and building his own, some of them with sixty oars and swifter and steadier than those of the Vikings. With nine of these ships the English won a modest naval victory off the South coast in 896. 'And this year', records the Chronicle with a sigh of relief, 'the host dispersed, some to East Anglia, some to Northumbria; and those without stock got themselves ships and sailed south oversea to the Seine.'

This distinction on the chronicler's part between the settlers returning to the Danelaw and 'those without stock'—those whom either necessity or inclination forced to sail overseas—is a very significant one. The same choice had been available in 879, but now the tide of settlement was running stronger than that of mere raiding. True, the Danes and Norwegians in East Anglia, Mercia, Northumbria and Cumbria were still only first-generation settlers, still able to mobilize, still a conquering army living under arms among a foreign population. But their compact military organization was loosening as their attachment to their farms increased. Between two such similar races as the English and Scandinavian, intercourse and intermarriage must have occurred very early on. In most material things the Viking settler differed little from his Anglian cousin who had preceded him, though the latter was ahead in agriculture and perhaps cattle-rearing because he had assimilated the farming methods established in Britain by the Romans. Already the first generation of settlers' children (many with English mothers) was coming of age in the only land it had known. Alfred's successors still had to plough a long hard furrow; but, in England at least, the era of settlement and integration had begun.

Elsewhere too in western Europe, the desire to raid was giving way to an even stronger urge to settle. In the late ninth century Harald Fairhair was beginning his long reign, and his unification of Norway set in motion several Viking enterprises. Some of these—such as the settlement of his native Iceland by Norwegians—are described by the later historian Snorri Sturluson in his *Heimskringla* and other writings, for example the saga of Rollaug, Hrolf or Rollo who was raiding in northern France from *c*. 885 onwards and who was certainly joined by some of those stockless or moneyless Vikings who sailed from England to the Seine in 896. According to Snorri: 'Hrolf was one of the three sons of Ragnvald, Jarl of Möre, King Harald's dearest friend; [he it was who cut off the hair which had been uncut and uncombed for ten years and gave him his by-name, Harald Fairhair.] Hrolf was a great Viking; he was grown so big that no steed could bear him and he therefore walked everywhere; he was called Hrolf the Ganger' (i.e. walker). For making a *strandhögg*, or shore-raid, in Norway king Harald declared him outlaw and thus set him off on his raiding career on more southerly coasts. The account of the English historian William of Malmes-

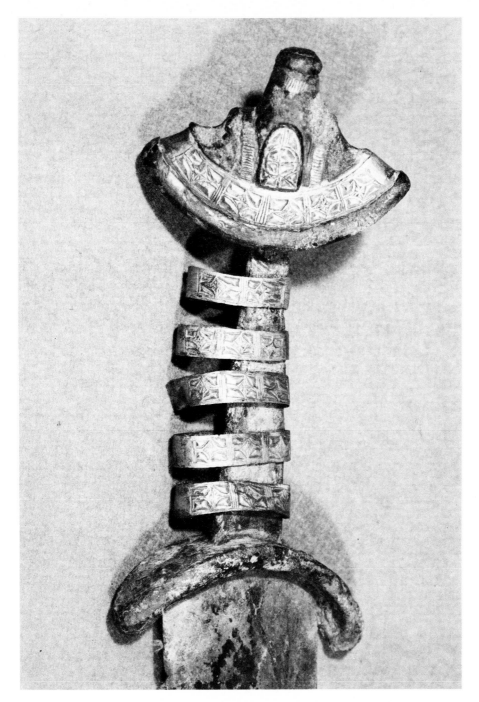

A Viking sword found in Northumbria. It stands waist high, is double-bladed and has the rare extravagance of five bands of silver on its handle.

bury agrees with this. Hrolf crossed to the Hebrides and Scotland (where he married a Scottish Christian wife) and thence to France, perhaps arriving there about 905. 'He harried there and possessed himself of a great jarldom; he settled many Norsemen there and it was afterwards called Normandy.' As we shall see, the evidence of personal names shows that the bulk of Hrolf's army was almost certainly Danish; many of them had come to Normandy via England. One thing reasonably certain is the date 911 by which Hrolf and his Vikings ceased their harrying and settled down to possess and cultivate the rich soil of Normandy.

Chapter IV   **Colonization**

> When Denmark's Raven soared on high,
> Triumphant through Northumbrian sky,
> Till, hovering near, her fatal croak
> Bade Reged's Britons dread the yoke,
> And the broad shadow of her wing
> Blackened each cataract and spring,
> Where Tees in tumult leaves his source,
> Thundering o'er Cauldron and High Force:
> Beneath the shade the Northmen came,
> Fixed on each vale a Runic name.

Thus Sir Walter Scott, opening Canto IV of his verse-novel *Rokeby*, written in the full flood of early nineteenth-century Romanticism. Although the study of place-names, and of the runic alphabet, let alone of 'Runic Names' had evidently not progressed far by 1812, Scott's touch is, as so often, nevertheless a happy one. For it is precisely by the names the Northmen 'fixed on each vale' that historians are best able to assess their impact on those various parts of western Europe in which they formed permanent settlements. This is especially true of England and south Wales and of Normandy, and it is therefore with the study of place-names that much of this chapter will be concerned.

Where they happen to exist, early, or better still, contemporary, historical sources, are a most valuable form of evidence; so are coins and archaeological material. But both these latter are far more plentiful in the Vikings' homelands than in the lands they colonized. In Sweden alone some 30,000 Anglo-Saxon coins have been found, the fruits of Danegeld: but except in the case of Viking York the evidence of coinage in the story of Viking Britain is minimal. And while the three northern lands between them can produce well over 4,000 runic inscriptions (the only kind of Scandinavian document that is truly contemporary) Britain can provide a few dozen only, and these almost entirely in the North and West.

The testimony of another type of evidence—blood groups—might have shed much light on Viking settlements if only it had been possible to assemble consistent data from the countries concerned a little earlier in the twentieth century than was actually the case: say from 1914 when populations were still relatively stable, rather than from 1939 onwards. Although not perhaps entirely conclusive, an example of the sort of evidence blood groups can provide has been advanced in connection with the Viking settlement of Dyfed.

So, with other sources more or less defective, it is above all to place-names that we must turn for our evidence of Viking colonization as far as Britain and Normandy are concerned. However, before we do so, let us look at a third country once peopled by the Northmen, where the conditions under which settlement took place and the surviving evidence for this settlement are both unique. This country is Iceland, called by early geographers 'Thule' but, as one of them remarks, 'known to few people because of its remoteness'.

Iceland and the Atlantic

During the seventh and eighth centuries Irish monks and anchorites in search of solitude braved the northern seas in their curraghs and reached—a few of them—the Orkneys, Shetlands and Faroes, getting to Iceland by about the year 800.

Isolation, together with a relative freedom from, or even disdain of, aristocratic and royal tenets allowed Iceland—at least until the mid-thirteenth century—to develop as a democratic (some would say aristo-democratic) parliamentary commonwealth, and, indeed, to become the first true republic in modern Europe. In Greenland too, settled largely from Iceland, the government was based on the Icelandic model.

Carried out on the principle of 'first come first served' the physical settlement of Iceland was a straightforward affair of individual initiative, an eye for a likely piece of territory together with the strength to appropriate it and subsequently hold it against all comers. Successful emigration then, as in all ages, depended on careful planning at the home-base: building or buying ships, fitting them up and loading them with families, retainers, slaves, livestock, supplies of food and drink, tools and weapons. This was an enterprise requiring not just initiative and planning ability but considerable capital resources also; once a family had become rich enough to fit out a Viking ship, it must have added wealth to wealth, besides enormously increasing its prestige. Since the main stream of Iceland's immigrants came from just those provinces of south-west Norway (Sogn, Hordaland, Rogaland) with the longest traditions of Viking piracy, these capital resources—the means to acquire all these necessities—were more likely derived from loot than from profits of honest farming. Whatever the means by which it was achieved, the chief cause of the large-scale exodus from this particular part of Norway (the fjords from what is now Ålesund down to Stavanger) was, once again, precisely the same one that had sent its young men out a-viking eighty years previously: the inescapable fact that this region has, in proportion to its great extent, only a small amount of productive land and is cut off by mountains from any possibility of expansion to the north or east. Many powerful families (for example the jarls of Lade) were based on islands, whence it was easy to set out on expeditions.

To the early arrivals at least, the grass-covered expanses of Iceland must have seemed boundless. There were no limits to the amount of land each settler could appropriate and the pronouncement by Harald Fairhair, quoted in *Landnámabók* that 'no one should occupy more than he and his crew could carry fire around in one day' could only have been a dead letter in this new country where no royal writ ran.

A step by step narration of a much more leisurely and perhaps fairly typical 'land-taking' occurs in chapters 27 and 28 of Egil's Saga, written down (*c.* 1225) by Egil's own descendant the 'unreliable because creative', Icelandic historian Snorri Sturluson. In this account we see Egil's father, Skallagrim, staking his extensive claims along the Borgär fjord, north of Reykjavik, naming the various landmarks as he did so, 'and after he had allotted land to his ships' crews Skallagrim explored the territory still further inland'. It is instructive and evocative eleven centuries later (or seven and a half if one prefers the saga-date) to be able to pick up even a medium-scale map of modern Iceland and trace on it, through the place-names, the movements of this ninth-century Viking enterprise, so little have Icelandic names altered.

It may seem a paradox to ascribe to a people like the Vikings, with their reputation for getting what they wanted by violence and producing no better claim than the right of the strongest, a respect for law and order and for the principles of democracy. But the poacher turned gamekeeper is proverbial and however ill-gotten their gains (as for example in England and Normandy), once the Vikings had acquired them they were as ready as the next man to invoke the law in defending and securing their 'rights'. This volte-face occurred in all the countries colonized by the Vikings, but nowhere more noticeably than in Iceland, where the free-for-all land-grab ended and, within the space of a single year or so, the rule of law began.

The flow of land-hungry settlers ended for two reasons: the foremost being simply that all the best land had been taken up; another being that perhaps this island of icefields, fierce torrents and volcanic desert no longer appeared to be quite the wonderland the first enthusiastic pioneers back in the 870s had painted it. The rule of law—the ordering of affairs in the

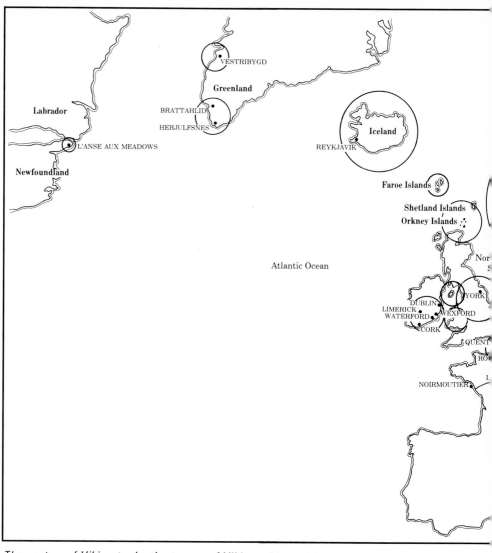

The centres of Viking trade, the targets of Viking raids and (circled) the main areas of Viking colonization.

common interest so that men could live in harmony—began with the setting up of the Althing in 930 'and thereafter men had but one law here in the land'.

To say 'inside every robber Viking was a law-abiding, indeed litigious, citizen trying to get out' is doubtless to overstate the case and ignore the many incorrigible ones; but there is no denying the respect for law common to the Germanic and Scandinavian peoples. 'With laws shall our land be built up but with lawlessness wasted away', says the wise and peace-loving Njal, and a preoccupation with justice common to all the Viking lands has survived down the centuries.

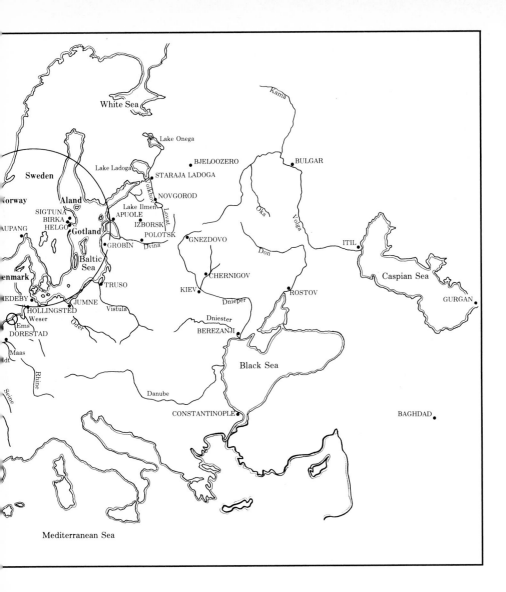

In Iceland during the settlement period law-giving had been in the hands of the scattered local communities each under its chief land-owner who would very often also perform the functions of a priest. These chieftains now joined themselves together to form a general assembly, the Althing, held for two weeks every year on 'Thingvellirsletten', the assembly plains some 30 miles east of Reykjavik. To begin with, the Althing was both parliament and judgement seat, a legislative and judicial body. The power, as might be expected, resided in the hands of the priest-chieftains (*godar*) themselves, 39 leading men of hereditary influence and wealth who in turn elected their president or law-speaker.

The code of laws they administered was imported from those same south-western provinces of Norway from which the Icelanders had come, with modifications suited to the needs of the new colony. Only parts of the original code have survived, but, as was general at this period, much reference would be made to human life and property and offences against them, each injury being precisely equated with its penalty. The laws of Iceland and the laws of the Danelaw in England have much in common.

The first two centuries of the Althing (930–1130) were also the time when the events later written down in the Icelandic sagas were actually taking place. The sagas abound in legal formulae and terminology—some of it perhaps inaccurately recollected—and it is clear, from the amount of space allocated to them, that judicial procedure and forensic matters in general were subjects of prime interest to these early medieval Norsemen. They held the place occupied in later centuries by theological discussion and later still by the niceties of the football match. The only contemporary themes to be dealt with at length, and with the same loving care for detail, are those of battle and death: ringside commentaries describing the exact blows struck by sword or halberd and the angles at which arms and heads fly off occur throughout the sagas. Grim though it is, the subject is not infrequently treated with wry humour: 'Kolskegg whirled around and leapt at him, swung at his thigh with the short-sword and cut off Kol's leg. "Did that one land or not?" asked Kolskegg. "That's my reward for not having my shield", said Kol. He stood for a moment on one leg, looking down at the stump. "You don't need to look", said Kolskegg. "It's just as you think—the leg is off!" '

In Iceland the change from paganism to Christianity was as sudden and dramatic as the adoption of law and centralized government had been seventy years before. The new religion was adopted by the island in 1000, the year of the millennium whose approach had been viewed with doubt and surmise by many medieval folk, both Christians and those on the fringe of Christianity.

For at least 20 years before this, missionaries from England and Saxony had been preparing the ground, and Iceland's first historian, Ari the Learned, tells of many families in the island who willingly received the faith from them. He mentions one—and there were no doubt others—with a Christian tradition stretching back for four generations; their home, significantly, was one of the several farmsteads in the sagas with the name Kirkjubær—'the place with a church'. The devout convert Ketil 'the Foolish' earned his nickname from pagan neighbours because he called his farm by this name.

But it was the Icelanders themselves, sponsored by the Norwegian king, who finally effected the country's conversion. Landing 'in the eleventh week of summer' in the year 1000, two missionaries named Gizur and Hjalti rallied round them a number of the island's Christian inhabitants and proceeded to the Althing. On the other side those who still clung to the worship of Odin and Thor also massed their forces.

The preserver of the peace was Lawspeaker Thorgeir, himself a pagan, who, after a day of meditation beneath his cloak, got both Christians and heathens alike to pledge their acceptance of his ruling, whatever it might be, 'for an impossible situation arises if we do not all have one and the same law; if the laws are divided the peace will be divided and we cannot tolerate that.'

Thorgeir then made his declaration: that all men in the land should henceforth be Christian and renounce the worship of idols, and other heathen practices. 'The pagans', says Ari, 'felt they had been grossly betrayed; but despite that the new faith became law.'

For the next two and a half centuries this Viking colony flourished as an independent Christian democracy. True, such a phrase to some extent idealizes an actual state of society where life can never have been easy, whose independence was the result of its extreme remoteness and whose democracy was one in which, although all free men were equal, 'some were a great deal more equal than others'. But, having said this, we have to concede that the Iceland of 'Sagatiden' and 'Sturlungetiden' (1000–1250) displayed certain unique qualities and achievements.

The Icelanders' genius—the word is not too strong—lay in diverse directions. First, and not least, in getting themselves an adequate living from harsh land and a stormy ocean; and secondly in exploration in all directions across that ocean. Not only were links maintained with Norway and Europe in the east but they pushed west and north as well, discovering Spitzbergen, Jan Mayen and Greenland which was colonized on the Icelandic model with settlements which, between their founding in the 980s and their eventual extinction around 1500, may have reached a population of 3,000 or more. Finally, and of this there can be no doubt, Icelanders explored, and for a brief few years settled on, the north-eastern corner—Labrador and Newfoundland—of the continent of America.

But the talents of these Icelanders were not all geared to physical activity. Their third claim to genius, and no doubt the one by which the world best remembers them, lies in the field of literature, for which this primitive little country developed a surprising and outstanding faculty. No account of the Vikings in Iceland, however cursory, can be complete without a glance at the literary output which followed their settlement of the island. For a population of pioneer stock, probably never numbering more than 60,000 and living at the world's end, this output is remarkable, both for its quality and its quantity.

The literature divides into three categories, of which the most characteristically Icelandic is the saga. For many people nowadays this word has come to mean a prose or verse epic dealing with heroic and warlike achievements—especially one involving the Gods of Valhalla, or other

Viking settlement in Iceland at the turn of the 10th century was followed in 930 by establishment of a republican law adapted from the Norwegian code. A national assembly was held each year north-east of Reykjavik on the lava-strewn plains at Thingvellir (below). Here the people gathered in 1000 and agreed to accept Christianity. Iceland was base for expeditions that discovered Greenland and America. The crosier (left) comes from a Greenland settlement.

mythical beings. The famous *Beowulf* is an Old English saga of this legendary kind.

Though the typical Icelandic saga, of which about forty survive, was also 'heroic' the heroes it dealt with were not mythical beings but actual individuals, men and women rooted firmly in the history and geography of Iceland itself and of the other countries of western Europe, and, since sagas were above all family biographies, the individual is always portrayed in his extended family context. In all the sagas the Scandinavian love of genealogical detail is given full scope. Without his pedigree a character scarcely exists—and sometimes the greatest villains have the longest pedigrees!

In their original form the sagas were recited as entertainment at feasts and gatherings. After a few generations (*c.* 1020–1120) their content became accepted and fixed. During the next century the sagas were written down, which stylized them still further. Finally, between 1220 and 1360, the material was amplified, polished and sometimes grouped together. The earliest surviving manuscripts date from slightly later still.

The sagas in their present form are therefore to some extent 'emotion recollected in tranquillity', and we need to remind ourselves that in the poetic process a good many actual events of the tenth century have been rationalized and tidied up to conform with the conditions and outlook of the fourteenth. Those parts of the sagas that have come down to us in their least altered form are the verses, like the one on the Battle of Brunanburh quoted later in this chapter.

Apart from these verses the sagas were epics in prose: poetry as such forms the second category of Icelandic literature. This art stood in the same relation to cultivated Icelanders as music did to Elizabethan England—scarcely a prominent Icelander but knew how to turn a rhyme. The aim of the poet in most ages is to secure the greatest beauty of sound, and, to secure this, Icelandic poetry used many devices—rhyme, assonance, elaborate phraseology, and complex structure and ornament.

Eyvind Skaldaspillir ('skald-despoiler', so nicknamed because he once plagiarized someone else's poem) may stand as the typical Icelandic poet. Like many others he attached himself as official bard to a great man, in this case king Haakon the Good of Norway. Icelandic poetry dealt with many subjects—wars and battles, genealogy, mythology, religion. One of the best-known Icelandic poems *Völuspá* ('The Sybil's Prophecy') combines the latter two and gives us the clearest picture of pagan Viking beliefs.

Lastly, the Icelanders made a name for themselves as historians, especially the founder of their historical school, Ari the Learned (1067–1148). Ari's achievements would rate high in any age—a history of the kings of Norway down to 1066, the marvellously comprehensive *Landnámabók* already referred to and the *Islendingabók* on the ecclesiastical and civil history of Iceland (with a section on Greenland) down to 1127.

Bloodshed, feuding and slavery apart, this Viking community in its early centuries has much that is admirable: not least the spectacle of free men, owning their own land, making their own decisions—poets and visionaries who were yet neither too proud nor too impractical to labour themselves in their fields and their blacksmiths' shops. We must not discount the Celtic element—it was this blending of Irish with Norse that made the Icelanders greater than either—but if this is what a society of mainly Viking stock could achieve, cut off from the world and under conditions of peace and Christianity, must we not ask ourselves whether some revision of the traditional assessment of these people is not long-overdue?

England

We have followed the Viking attacks on England up to the end of the ninth century. Alfred the Great did not see that century out—his vast achievements were packed into a life span, comparatively short even for those days, of under fifty years. For good or ill it was he, more than any other single man, who secured England's survival as a Germanic state with Scandinavian connections rather than the other way round.

The succession in 899 of Alfred's son, Edward the Elder, saw little change in the established English tactic of setting up forts or strong points known as 'burhs' in which the local inhabitants and their cattle could be defended against raiding Danes and from which counter-attacks could be organized. The present-day city of Oxford has its origins in one of these new settlements, while Wallingford guarded a similar crossing lower down the Thames. This policy carried out by Edward on the borders of Wessex was matched further north in the English midlands by the king's sister Aethelflaed, 'Lady of the Mercians', and her husband, Ethelred, earl of Mercia. Chester, for example, which the Danes had attempted to occupy in the 890s remained a key site at the north-west corner of English territory and was attacked by both Norwegians and Danes from Ireland. Here, the old Roman fortifications were repaired by Aethelflaed in 907, but in many other instances—Tamworth, Stafford and Warwick, for example—burhs were set up on entirely new sites. By 920 Aethelflaed had won back from the Danes two of their 'Five Towns'—Derby and Leicester—together with the territories around them. The Vikings of York also made peace with her and bound themselves to obey her.

The whole tenor of the Anglo-Saxon chronicle during these years is of English advances even further north up the island; and this recovery by the Saxon kings of the southern Danelaw meant that by the date of Edward's death (924) all England south of the Trent was under their control, including areas thickly settled by the 'here', like East Anglia and Nottinghamshire.

The recovery of these areas by the English was undoubtedly made easier for them by the fact that, in becoming landowners and farmers, the

Vikings had surrendered much of the unity they had possessed as members of the 'here' under warrior chiefs (albeit temporary ones) in the old raiding days. Nor, in England, did they develop, in place of this wartime solidarity, the sort of political unity which marked their settlement of Normandy. Clearly the Danes did not regard having to recognize an English king as a very great calamity, so long as their own property and position in the country were secured.

Edward the Elder's successor was king Athelstan, who faced a rather different 'Viking question' from that of his father. Athelstan's problems lay no longer with the settled, agricultural and partly Christianized Danes of the southern Danelaw but with the still mainly pagan and mobile Norwegian Vikings of York, aided by their cousins from the Viking kingdom of Dublin. Beyond Danish Northumbria the territories of Anglian Northumbria were menaced by Norwegian Vikings, Danes (from the time of Halfdan's 876 settlement), Scots to the North and Britons of the kingdom of Strathclyde to the north-west.

It was against this unholy alliance that king Athelstan fought the battle of 937 known, among other names, as Brunanburh.

Brunanburh is an important landmark in English history because it broke the Norse-Celtic confederacy and prevented what might have been a lasting dismemberment of Cumbria and Northumbria, with a Norse kingdom firmly established from sea to sea and a border with Scotland running perhaps from the Solway Firth to the estuary of the Tees.

The Anglo-Saxon Chronicle celebrates the battle in what is perhaps the earliest outpouring of English patriotic verse—the 'Song of Brunanburh'. The poet tells how the defeated Scots and Norse

> ... left behind them, the carcases to share, the carrion to devour,
> The dusky plumaged crow, the black raven with horny beak
> The grey-feathered, white-tailed eagle
> And that gray beast, the wolf of the Wolds.

It is not at all surprising that both Scandinavian and Anglo-Saxon tradition and bardic legend should have preserved memories of this significant battle, a victory for the Anglo-Saxons that at once secured and advanced their overlordship of Northumbria.

King Athelstan, like his father and grandfather, had just the personal qualities—strength combined with generosity—to gain the respect and co-operation of his Scandinavian subjects, whose language he probably spoke, or at least understood. He was a friend of his contemporary fellow-rulers in Norway, Harold Finehair and his son Haakon the Good; indeed, the latter was brought up in the English court as Athelstan's foster son. Outside the Scandinavian world too, Athelstan was well connected; his sister Eadgiva was queen of France and she and her son the future Louis IV lived much at Athelstan's court, as did Alan of Brittany and one of king Constantine of Scotland's sons. The emperor Otto, and the rulers of Burgundy and Acquitaine were all brothers-in-law of the Anglo-Saxon 'king and Bretwalda of all these islands'.

Athelstan's death two years after Brunanburh was a temporary setback for the English cause, and one of which the Vikings took full advantage. But who, in the England of 939, could still strictly speaking be called 'Vikings'? No longer, clearly, the settlers of the Danelaw (many of whom by now were a loyal and integral part of the English realm), but their cousins and frequent enemies the 'white strangers' from Norway, or more generally from Norway via Ireland. These Dublin Norwegians were led by Olaf, descendant of the Ivar we met in chapter III, whose dynasty had, since the late ninth century, been styling themselves 'Kings of the Norsemen in the whole of Ireland and Britain'.

The complicated events of 942–954 centre on Northumbria and on its capital York, with various rulers of this Dublin dynasty on the Norse side contending with the short-lived English kings, Edmund, Edred and Edwy, younger brothers of Athelstan; this struggle is one of the episodes to which Viking York and its archaeology forms the background.

When the last of the Norwegian rulers of York, Harold Fairhair's son Eirik Bloodaxe, was finally driven out in 954 and killed (with five other Norse leaders) on the wild watershed of Stainmore there was peace in England for a generation, until the re-commencement of Viking raids under a new set of leaders and with a new purpose in 981.

It is now time to examine the actual settlements of the Scandinavians during the ninth and tenth centuries in the detail that their importance warrants. For these settlements were a turning point in the history of England and their effects would still be recognizable for centuries to come in the differences which defined the Anglo-Saxon and Anglo-Scandinavian sides of the country's character and language.

Settlements began in England in 876, no doubt partly because by this time the old-style raids had reduced the country to such poverty that they were no longer profitable. The first recorded partitions were carried out in the far north by the Danish leader Halfdan, son of Ragnar, 'who took with him one third of the pagan army occupying England and put into the Tyne with a strong fleet, moving near the mouth of the Team' [a small tributary of the Tyne]. 'And the settlers proceeded to till the land and gain their living thereby.' Following the example of many successful invaders they began to reap the fruits of the country they had injured.

The territory eventually settled by Halfdan—'Rex Haldanus Danamarchiae' as a chronicler calls him—corresponded more or less with modern Yorkshire, the areas of the East Riding, southern North Riding and eastern parts of the West Riding being those of the thickest Danish settlement. The

Land-hunger accounted for many of the Norwegian Viking ▶
expeditions overseas.

northern section (Bernicia) of Northumbria seems to have remained Anglian.

There are various methods by which an invading army can effect a settlement in an already inhabited territory. The first and most drastic way is to kill and drive out a high percentage of the population in the countryside or town in question. This (according to the Anglo-Saxon Chronicle) is what the Danes did in Wessex during their attempt to occupy it during the winter of 877–8. The enormity of these tactics provoked the Anglo-Saxons to a resistance so powerful that it threw the Vikings out of Wessex for ever.

The next method is to subjugate the inhabitants of a district so thoroughly that their land and possessions can be taken over and themselves retained as the slaves of the conquerors. This is perhaps what happened when the Danish host shared out part of Mercia in the autumn of 877. The reaction here may account for the relative scantiness of Scandinavian settlement in this region, and the ease with which the English forces reclaimed it during the years after 900.

The third method, probably the one most frequently used in England, and certainly the way most likely to lead to successful and permanent integration, is settlement with a measure of mutual consent and agreement between the newcomers and the existing inhabitants. The systematic occupation of East Anglia from 879 onwards, carried out by the section of the Danish army led by Guthrum, was accompanied by a treaty between two equal powers, and its spirit of equality extended right down the classes of settler and host alike. Under 'Guthrum's Peace', his English subjects, though technically the defeated race, were in no way discriminated against: the Anglian churl still farmed his own land, and his 'wergild', or worth in the eyes of the law, was the same as that of his Danish peasant counterpart.

The amalgamation of Viking and Anglian stocks in East Anglia (Norfolk and Suffolk), in Essex and in the Anglian areas immediately to the west (Cambridgeshire, Huntingdonshire and Bedfordshire) appears to have been a thorough one. In most cases the newcomers adopted the existing place-names; compared with the adjacent Danelaw counties of Leicestershire, Nottinghamshire and Lincolnshire the incidence of Scandinavian names in Guthrum's territory is relatively small. In Essex there are two only.

Guthrum himself (he died in 889) has the distinction of being the first Viking to be mentioned by the Anglo-Saxon Chronicle in anything like affectionate terms: 'And Guthrum, the northern King, whose baptismal name was Athelstan, passed away: he was King Alfred's godson, and he dwelt in East Anglia, and was the first to take possession of that country.' Guthrum evidently took his conversion seriously: he used his Christian name 'Edeltan' on his coins in preference to his pagan one, and was no doubt a powerful influence in the Christianizing of his fellow countrymen.

We have looked at the methods of settlement in territory already inhabited. Where it occurs in an uninhabited (e.g. Iceland) or only sparsely

◄ *Scandinavian settlement in Greenland gave way to a worsening climate, and to the Eskimos, by the end of the 14th century.*

populated region the invaders' tactics are rather different. Spare land can be taken up without dispossessing existing occupants. In the absence of natives to work for them the invaders (unless they bring in slaves) must labour for themselves. This was the case in the first, far northern settlement of 876 when Halfdan's settlers 'tilled the ground and gained their living thereby', and probably also in much of Danish Northumbria settled during the next half century by Halfdan and his successors.

In these 'Counties of broad acres'—the later Yorkshire and Lincolnshire—there was enough elbow room for the development of those territorial units peculiar (in the whole of England) to areas settled by the Scandinavian armies. These are the 'sokes', and are the organization by which, more than anything else, the Viking soldier was—over a large part of the Danelaw—transformed into a respectable English farmer.

We can observe what seems to be an early example of a soke coming into existence in the account of the Durham chronicler Symeon. Recording the year 912 he relates how the Viking leader Rognvald cleared a piece of territory of its inhabitants and partitioned it between two of his military leaders: 'And the one part, to the south, he gave to a certain powerful soldier called Scula, from the village called (Castle) Eden to the one called Billingham; the other portion, lying between (Castle) Eden and the river Wear he gave to a man called Onlafball'. It is related of this same Olaf Ballr ('the stubborn') that he dropped down dead in Chester-le-Street church after invoking Thor and Odin against St. Cuthbert and that these lands thereupon became part of St. Cuthbert's territory and the nucleus of the county of Durham.

Each of these army officers thus received a tract of land about twelve miles long by several miles wide—the typical dimensions of a soke—and they in turn would subdivide these areas among all those serving under them that wished to settle down on the land in preference to continuing their Viking career. As the historian F. M. Stenton says: 'It was almost inevitable that the rank and file of this army, who are known to have kept their military organisation long after they had turned from war to agriculture, should group themselves upon the soil under the leaders who had brought them to England.'

As might therefore be expected, these sokes occur in just those parts of England settled by the Scandinavians, but nowhere else in the country; for example Leicestershire, which was part of Danish Mercia had these districts, while in neighbouring Warwickshire, lying in English Mercia, they do not appear at all.

Sokes occur in all shapes and sizes: the soke of Kirton in north Lincolnshire extends from Scunthorpe southward for about ten miles in a comparatively narrow strip. Further south, the soke of Greetham was originally spread over thiry-five villages. Almost adjoining it is the best-known example of all, and one that has survived on the maps of today—the soke of Peterborough. This is an irregular lozenge, with sides of six or seven miles. The complicated and varied nature of sokes makes it likely that they had grown over a long period rather than that they had been created by any act of legislation.

The settlers living in these districts were free men, owning their own holdings and with a long-surviving loyalty to their comrades-in-arms and to their erstwhile leaders. These holdings, again, varied greatly in size, and perhaps reflect the status in the invading army of the first recipient at the original shareout. The farms held by these sokemen seem on the whole to have been larger in the northern Danelaw and smaller in East Anglia, where by the time of the Domesday Book (1086) many descendants of these Danish peasants were, though still free landowners, living on small holdings of only one to twenty acres. But this may have been the result of the recurring subdivision of land under different laws of inheritance.

Although only a portion of the land settled by the Vikings was organized into sokes, a more general division of English territory was also taking place during the tenth century, probably initiated by king Athelstan. This was the organization of the whole country south of the Mersey and Humber into shires or counties, and the further subdivision of these counties into 'hundreds' which in theory were the areas occupied by one hundred families, each on its 'hide' (40–100 acres) of land. The establishment throughout so much of England of this uniform scheme of local administration was a tribute to the supremacy of Wessex and her kings throughout so much of the land.

In the counties of the northern Danelaw (and including one example in County Durham), the equivalent of the hundred was called the 'wapentake', a term which came into currency in the second half of the tenth century. In this too, the Danelaw betrays its army origins, so different from the individual settlements recorded in Iceland's *Landnámabók*, since the old Norse word *vápnatak* was originally the way a body of armed men showed their consent to legislative or other decision by waving or brandishing their weapons. In England it quickly came to be identified with the actual territorial division to which these ex-soldiers and their descendants belonged and to which they owed their immediate allegiance.

For many centuries to come these wapentakes (or 'hundreds' in the East Anglian section of the Danelaw) remained the fundamental territorial units on which local government and local justice were based. In Yorkshire and Lindsey (the northern section of Lincolnshire) another Scandinavian term appears. This is the Riding, the 'thirding' or third part into which these counties were divided for administration purposes. Each Riding contained a number of wapentakes.

Riding and wapentake are general terms: as we noted at the beginning of this chapter, it is the multitude of individual Scandinavian place-names that really gives us our knowledge of the Danelaw settlements, telling us, for example, that its eastern parts were largely Danish, its north-western area was settled by Norwegians from Ireland, and its centre by both streams.

The Viking settlements of Britain and Normandy, as of the Baltic lands and Russia are an area of history where irrefutable archaeological evidence, conclusive blood-group frequencies or even some moderately reliable contemporary chroniclers would be welcome indeed! As it is, place-name and other linguistic studies have to be stretched to fill a rather wide gap. Can the nationality of settlers (whether they were Danish or Norwegian for instance) be deduced from their evidence? Were the numerous places in Britain with Scandinavian names really founded by Vikings at all, or do they simply represent existing Anglo-Saxon or Celtic settlements re-named under Scandinavian influence? At least one Scandinavian writer thinks that many personal names commonly accepted as Anglian, and which have formed 'typical Anglian' place-names in -ingham and -ington, are in fact Old Norse personal names. The whole subject is at present under vigorous discussion by scholars in different countries and many assumptions are being questioned.

In England the commonest Scandinavian place-name elements are -by and -thorpe, both meaning farmstead or settlement. 'By' is found all over Scandinavia and features in over 700 English place-names, sometimes as the name of an individual farm but more often as a settlement shared by several households and made up of several farms or dwellings—what we should now call a village. In Norway and Iceland, by contrast, it is used for a single farm. 'By' is usually compounded with another element which can either be a feature of the landscape or a work of man or, most commonly of all, a personal name.

'Thorpe' which was originally a Germanic word (*dorf*) is common in Denmark, and hence in England, but rarely occurs in Iceland or Norway. In the Viking settlements of Normandy it takes the form *tourp*. Its original meaning was probably 'a gathering' and, as compared with 'by', it generally implies a secondary settlement or one in an outlying situation.

The coincidence of parishes and other places in England having names of Scandinavian origin with the area of the Danelaw itself is remarkably exact. Only a handful of such places lies south or west of Watling Street (today's A.5) and in the whole mass of Saxon southern England scarcely a Scandinavian name is to be found. A tiny exception near the North Sea coast of Essex is formed by the parishes of Thorpe and Kirby le Soken. Other apparently 'thorpe' names outside the Danelaw, for example Heythrop and Cokethorpe in Oxfordshire, indicate that 'thorpe' as a place-name element had already reached that part of the Continent from which the Saxons themselves emigrated to England.

As we shall see, there was a close similarity between the speech of the Anglian north of England and the Old Norse spoken by the various Viking invaders. There seems also to have been a much greater degree of acceptance

The Scandinavian settlement of the north of England involved considerable intermingling of ideas. The heathen practice of burial with full panoply of arms is portrayed on a Viking's tomb-stone in Yorkshire (right), and on the back is a pagan dragon, but the cross itself is nothing if not Christian. A hoard of silver, buried in about 920 near York and including these magnificent pieces (below)—the pin is 19 cms long—testifies, however, to someone's fear for his property in a time of continuing political instability.

The blacksmith who fitted out this church door at Stillingfleet in Yorkshire had a clear idea of the lines of a Viking ship.

94

of the newcomers there—an acceptance which, allied to a suspicion of the growing power of Wessex, not infrequently linked together the Anglian and Viking populations of northern England against the Saxon southerners. However, though this particular assimilation has blurred some of the distinctions between the two groups, there are still plenty of place-names quite undoubtedly indicating Viking settlement. The Vikings in the north of England gave to the natural features of the landscape the names they had been accustomed to using in their own countries: beck (for stream), dale, gill and slack (for the larger and smaller valleys), foss (for waterfall), carr (for marshy ground) or holm (for islet of dry land).

Among the works of man, they applied thwaite to a forest clearing, garth to a small enclosure and toft to a plot with a building.

The Norwegian practice—still to be observed there—of grazing upland dairy pastures in summer time only and living in *saeter* (temporary huts or sheds) for the season has given rise to a large number of names in 'sett' or 'side' (Countersett, Ossett, Gunnerside). *Skali*, a Scandinavian word of similar meaning, has produced names in '-scales', '-sgill' and '-skill': Windscale and Seascale are perhaps the best-known of these. Names in 'erg', which is the equivalent term in old Irish, were introduced by the Norwegian settlers from Ireland: Sizergh, Torver, Mansergh are examples.

'Cros' or 'kross' was a Viking word-form replacing both 'rood' and 'cruc', the existing Anglo-Saxon terms for the symbol of Christianity. From being at first a recognizably Irish-Norwegian importation it spread all over the North and Midlands of England as the common word, in speech as well as place-names and eventually, from the fifteenth century onwards, became the accepted term in the English language.

Some place-names from the Viking colonization denote the settlers' actual nationality. One cluster of these includes the 'Irbys', 'Irebys', 'Irtons' and others containing the Norse term *Iri* for an Irishman. We must remind ourselves that the name of a place is not generally given to it by its own inhabitants but rather by those of the next community. The occurrence of 'Dan-' or 'Norman-' in a place-name is not only a fair indication that the inhabitants of that place were reckoned by their neighbours to be Danes or Norwegians, but is also some sort of assessment of the rarity or otherwise of the particular nationality involved. Clearly, in districts of heavy Danish settlement like north Lincolnshire or the East Riding one does not expect to find names in 'Dan-'. But it is in precisely such areas where the Norwegian was something of a rarity that village names like Normanby, and (hybrid form) Normanton, occur. These hybrids—Scandinavian names followed by 'tun' or a similar Anglian ending may indicate the partial re-naming of an existing 'tun' simply by substituting the name of the new Viking owner for that of the dispossessed Englishman. Other place-names in the Danelaw which indicate the original settler's racial origin are those with the element Bret- or Ingle-, by which the Scandinavian majority denoted the presence amongst them of isolated settlements of Britons (i.e. the Welsh of Strathclyde) and native Englishmen respectively. There are also a few place-names incorporating the actual word 'Viking'—whether as a personal name or as an epithet. Wigston near Leicester and Wigginton outside York are two of these. Illustrating Viking social structure, Lazenby is the settlement of the *leysing* or freedman, Bonby that of the *bondi* or small peasant who may or may not be free, and Threlkeld the spring of the thræll who certainly was not.

Among the most interesting names in the Viking settlement are those which contain the element 'thing', the word for the assembly or local council of the inhabitants. Often it is associated with a word like 'field' or 'hill' and in this form in England denotes the actual meeting place of a hundred or wapentake. These council fields or hills—thingwalls or thinghows—are scattered all over the Scandinavian world. The most celebrated ones are the Thingvellir of Iceland, which we have already seen, and the Tynwald court on the Isle of Man, both of which have survived until the present day. Others can still be found on the map of Britain from Suffolk up to Shetland.

A great many place-names incorporate an actual individual whose personal name is Scandinavian in origin. The old North Riding of Yorkshire is an area where the Dano-Norwegian displacement was probably as thorough as anywhere in the whole Danelaw. In its place-names we can identify over 220 different Scandinavian personal names, many of them occurring more than once, and in the neighbouring East Riding there are, in addition to these, a further 89. Even a county like Derbyshire, on the fringe of the Danelaw, produces 24 Scandinavian (mainly Danish) personal names.

Taken in the mass, the great variety of these men's and women's names is striking. Many of them are of a descriptive, mock-descriptive or nickname character. Moreover, with minor variations, the same names are to be found distributed over the whole Viking world.

Of these old Norse names a few have survived down the centuries as 'Christian' names in use today. Many more, their original form obscured by centuries of change, must be looked to as the ancestors of hundreds of our modern Danelaw surnames, which have, of course, spread from there all over Britain and all over the world. A good example (one could adduce dozens more) is the name 'Toki'. Unrecognizable in its Viking form, and no longer in use as either a personal name or a surname, it is nevertheless the original from which all our present-day families of Tock, Tuck, Tooke, Tuke, Tookey—and doubtless several more—derive their ancient surname.

Although, as we have seen, the southern limits of the Danelaw are clearly demarcated, its northern frontier is less easy to define. Most historians place the boundary between Danish Northumbria and Anglian Northumbria on the river Tees, but the course of this river is very erratic and a more probable boundary to the Viking area of influence is to be found in the Roman road crossing this part of Northumbria in a north-easterly direction to join the north-south Roman road known as Dere Street; eastward from this junction to Tees-mouth a scatter of Scandinavian village names occurs along the north bank of the river. Place-name evidence supports this boundary, for at a point where the road traverses the watershed stands the ancient boundary mark Rey Cross (old Norse *rá*, a boundary), and adjoining the road in its eastward course are Ravock, Rowe Gill, Ray Gill and Raby, the last a site and castle associated in the eleventh century with king Knut. Along the same road there is a recurrence of the Viking personal name Steinn, in Stainmore (scene of Eirik Bloodaxe's last stand), Stainton and Staindrop by Raby, all perhaps commemorating some Viking guardian of this northern frontier.

A frontier it certainly was, since between here and Caithness on the north-east tip of Britain stretched territories where Angles, Scots and Picts seemed to have remained in possession of their lands largely undisturbed by the Vikings, apart from a narrow coastal strip where a scatter of place-names in 'haven' and 'ness' (headland) occurs. In the southern section, what is now Durham, Northumberland, Berwickshire and the Lothians was ruled in virtual independence by a number of ealdormen based on fastnesses like Bamburgh. Up in east Caithness, however, ruled by its jarls until the thirteenth century, the Norse names re-appear on the map—terminations in gill, wick, toft and ster (*stathr*, dwelling) are common and Thurso, its capital, named for Thor, still has a cross with a runic inscription. Rounding Cape Wrath (old Norse *hvarf*, a turning point) the inhospitable western coastline of Sutherland—the 'southern land' (as compared with Orkney and Shetland)—and Ross were without doubt visited by Norwegian Vikings. As in Ireland, Scandinavian place-names in these two counties have largely been obliterated, rather than assimilated, by the Gaelic, though Dingwall has remained the chief place of assembly in Ross and Cromarty, and rivers like the Brora and Laxford retain the Norse words for 'bridge' and 'salmon' respectively.

Two hundred miles further down the west coast is Galloway, another area of Scandinavian settlement. Here in the ninth century the native Gaels made common cause with Norwegian Vikings reputedly under Olaf the White who features so frequently in saga tradition. Under him and his successors Galloway remained relatively independent of the newly-unified Scotland for over two centuries. Galloway has numerous place-names in 'holm' and 'dale' and Wigtown is 'the settlement on the *vik*'.

On the deeply indented coastline of west Scotland, from the Mull of Galloway up to the Hebrides, are a number of 'Tarbets' and 'Tarberts', places where one stretch of water is separated from another merely by a narrow isthmus of land. The seagoing Scandinavians were experts at portage, dragging or carrying their boats across these necks of land to save many miles of sea voyage or to suprise the enemy. Indeed 'tarbet' is regarded by some as a Scandinavian word, a simple combination of the Norwegian *ta* (take or carry) and *bat* (boat). The protagonists of Gaelic prefer *tair* (across) and *beart* (bearing)—the whole word meaning an isthmus, since all the places where this 'bearing across' was done were, ipso facto, isthmuses. Whether they named them or not, those portage places were certainly much used by the Vikings; a classic case is recorded at Loch Lomond Tarbet when king Magnus Barefoot dragged his ships from the loch across to the head of Loch Long, at the end of the Viking period.

Midway from the Solway Firth to Dublin lies the Isle of Man. Its central position in the Irish Sea made it a target for raids from the early ninth century onwards, and it soon became a Viking colony. In the early tenth century the stream of Irish-Norse emigration from Ireland to north-west England began to flow and the Isle lay right in the path of this. There is no doubt about Man's strong Norse heritage and the place-name evidence partially substantiates this. Though this evidence is not of the overwhelming kind found in the English Danelaw, the Isle of Man has its fells in the hilly interior (Snaefell being the highest), wicks (*viks*) round the coastline, and a number of villages ending in -by and -dale. There is a virtual absence of pre-Viking Celtic names.

But it is in other evidence that Man is rich, especially compared with England; 11 Viking graves have been discovered against 16 in England and Wales and 40 stone carved crosses have yielded 29 runic inscriptions. These inscriptions name 44 individuals, 22 of whom are Scandinavians and 11 Irish.

The Isle of Man was under the rule of the Norse kings of Dublin until the late tenth century and thus was in direct communication with Norway, Dublin and York. From about 990 it came under the sway of the powerful jarls of Orkney and so owed allegiance to Norway; because of this it was pillaged by Svein Forkbeard, king of Denmark, in 994.

Wales

Our survey of Viking settlements in Britain would be incomplete without some further reference to two coastal areas, both in South Wales, which were undoubtedly colonized by Norwegians and Danes. These are the peninsulas of Gower and Dyfed, where distinct groups of Scandinavian place-names are to be found, both on the coast itself and inland. Although some Welsh historians dismiss any idea of permanent Norse settlements in their country, both place-names and sagas seem to indicate that these did take place. Wales, like Man, was in the centre of the zone of Viking activities and its disunity in the ninth and tenth centuries would have provided favourable conditions for raiding and settling. Like other Celtic areas, Wales was ambivalent about the Vikings. At the one extreme all the Welsh kings, around 880, commended themselves to Alfred the Great as their

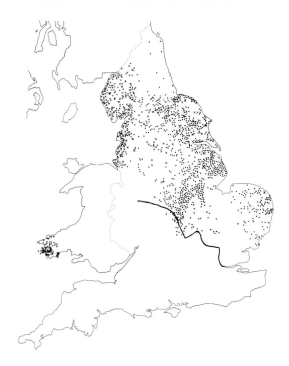

Scandinavian and Irish-Norwegian place-names have been located in profusion in England within the Danelaw (its southern limit marked here with a heavy line). Viking settlement in south-west Wales is a possibility supported by the number of Scandinavian names that can also be plotted there.

Saxon overlord (a precedent not neglected by later English kings!), at the other, its bards harped on 'the omen of Great Britain'—the day when an alliance of Scandinavians and Irish with Welsh of Wales, Cornwall and Strathclyde would together win a glorious victory over the Saxons and drive them out of Britain. Unfortunately the construction of Offa's Dyke (*c.* 790) had firmly cut these latter three off from each other and made this part of the alliance unworkable!

Historical evidence for this period is rather defective. The Welsh Annals (*Brut y Tywysogion*) were written down only in the twelfth century and lack the immediacy—and continuity—of the Anglo-Saxon Chronicle. The annals record unsuccessful Viking raids on Gower in 860, Hubba's activities in Dyfed in 877 and an invasion of 'black pagans' from across the Severn raiding and burning in east Wales in 893. Since nearly all the references are to dark strangers rather than white ones, Wales was probably in contact with *Daenysseit* or *gwyr Denmarc*; though Norsemen from Ireland must have navigated the western coasts and contributed names in -ey and -holm ('island') like Anglesey, Bardsey, Ramsey, Skokholm and Steepholm. In Gower we find Swansea (Sweinsey), (W)orms Head and Burry Holms. Norse merchants from Wales are known to have rallied at Dublin for the battle of Clontarf (1014) and in the following centuries documents reveal numbers of people with purely Scandinavian names living in the Vale of Glamorgan. In 1878 a typical Viking ship was found at the mouth of the Usk.

It is, however, Dyfed at the south-western tip of Wales that provides the strongest evidence for considerable and lasting Viking settlement. This evidence is fourfold; historical tradition, archaeological finds, place-names and blood groups.

From the Annals already cited we can premise that settlement in Dyfed, following raiding, might have increasingly occurred after about 870. From the known English parallels the newly powerful Wessex might be expected to take measures countering or controlling this movement at any time from the reign of Alfred. In fact the Anglo-Saxon Chronicle records successful operations by Edward the Elder against Scandinavian marauders off the South Wales coast in 915, after which 'they [the Vikings] went thence to Dyfed and then out to Ireland'.

In 921 king Edward sent an expedition to Milford Haven (in Anglo-Saxon 'Deepe stowe') and built a fort at 'Gladmuth', which must be the mouth of the Cleddau, the river whose twin branches divide Pembrokeshire. Long after this, in the 980s, a number of Danish raids on Dyfed are recorded, and the destruction of St. David's. In the late tenth and early eleventh century, according to the *Heimskringla*, the Norwegian kings Olaf Tryggvason and Olaf Haraldsson both ravaged Dyfed—perhaps an indication that by this time its inhabitants were mainly of Danish rather than Norwegian stock.

Archaeological finds from Dyfed of Viking date are, as in other instances, extremely rare; in their raiding and trading phase these seafarers would possibly leave very little mark on the land, and when they settled and farmed they were so assimilated into the existing culture as to once again leave few traces behind them. A small leaden tablet with an embossed inset of thin bronze was found on the shore of Freshwater Bay, and this, together with a single carved cross and the river Usk ship seem to be the only extant Viking antiquities from this region.

The scarcity of Scandinavian objects from south-west Wales is all the more striking alongside the abundance of place-name evidence, for nowhere else in Britain outside the Danelaw is there a district with so many names of Scandinavian origin. Round the coast, in addition to those already quoted, we find stacks and skerrys (*Emsger, Tusker*); -holms, nesses and eys; ports as purely Scandinavian in name as Tenby (Dan-by) or Fishguard (*Fiskigarthr*, the fishing garth) and its neighbouring Goodwick.

Round the shores of that vast land-locked harbour, Milford Haven, there are hybrids formed from Viking personal names: -Frey, Harald, Harding, Haakon, Herbrand, Thor, Ubbe and others. There is a Derby and a Colby, and the modern county town of Haverfordwest is named either from *haver* (oats) or Havardr's fjord.

In contrast to the number of names on its map, the present-day dialect of south Pembrokeshire (the north speaks Welsh) preserves only a handful of recognizably Scandinavian terms. But there is some further evidence indicating the survival for a thousand years of Norse influence on the genetic map of this remote corner of Britain. This evidence is based on the observation that where history shows populations to have a common origin they also have similar blood-group frequencies.

Statistics collected in the mid-twentieth century by the Blood Transfusion Service showed that the frequency of 'A' genes among the indigenous population of Pembrokeshire south of the Landsker was at levels noticeably higher than in the adjacent areas of Wales—levels up to 33.6 per cent, a figure not matched except in parts of Scandinavia.

The cautious conclusion is that this blood-group evidence does strengthen the probability that the Vikings established permanent settlements in 'Little England beyond Wales' and, moreover, that they probably also brought wives from Scandinavia; had they married Welshwomen the 'A' frequency would have been appreciably lower!

Normandy
We left the Viking leader Hrolf or Rollo seizing territories at the north-west corner of France, part of what was then known as 'Neustria'. This seizure was confirmed in 911 by Charles the Simple, king of France, in a treaty at St. Clair-sur-Epte. The territory ceded in 911 was only a small portion of the eventual dukedom of Normandy and centred on Rouen, which had been occupied a number of times by Viking forces during the previous half-century. In 924 a large additional area, Maine and Bessin, was added to this original nucleus. Rollo could now be styled 'Conqueror of Neustria' but, had it not been for the Vikings' immoderate greed for loot and the ability of the country to supply it, much more of the kingdom of the Franks might have become a Viking province.

Although, as we have seen, Rollo was probably a Norwegian, it is equally fairly certain that the majority of his fellow Vikings in Normandy came not from Norway but from Denmark, either direct or via the English Danelaw. The principal evidence for this has, once again, to be sought from the place-names; the only contemporary historians are Saxo Grammaticus and Dudo of St. Quentin with his rather legendary *Acts and Customs of the first Dukes of Normandy*. Saxo, author of *Deeds of the Danes*, is very little use on the subject of Normandy—according to him 'Northman' was just a *nom de guerre* that happened to be used by some Vikings! The sagas are not, of course, strictly contemporary, nor, being of Icelandic and Norwegian origin, can they be expected to shed much light on the settlement of Normandy, if it was essentially a Danish operation. We must even allow that Snorri Sturluson's account of duke Rollo's Norwegian origins *might* be the invention of a thirteenth-century patriotic historian: that it probably was *not* is helped by the fact that Rollo's daughter Gerløg, an undoubted historical personage, also bears a distinctly Norwegian name.

As usual the archaeological evidence for the Viking invasion and settlement of Normandy is sparse. A very few graves, a handful of brooches, a number of swords, spearheads and shield bosses (mostly from the rivers Seine and Loire)—this is all that seems to have survived from all the long decades of raiding in western Europe.

Archaeology and contemporary written records may contribute little to the story but place-names—hundreds of them—once again come to the historian's rescue. As was the case in England, place-names and the personal names of the settlers nearly all suffered a sea change on their voyage from Denmark. In Normandy this change is sometimes so great that the word is not easy to recognize. For example, the old Norse settlement name 'Kirkjubær' which survives in Iceland unaltered to the present day, and which in its English spelling 'Kirkby' is still fairly self-evident, becomes rather less so in the Norman version 'Carquebu'. In the same way 'thorp', unaltered as between England and Denmark, now acquires a Gallic flavour as 'tourp', as do Longuetuit and Braquetuit, the Norman versions of our familiar north of England Langthwaite and Brackenthwaite (modern Danish Langtved and Bregentved). 'Bekkr' in Normandy becomes -bec (Bolbec, Caudebec), 'holm' houlme, 'garth' gart and 'lund' londe. Other Viking place-name elements are '-topt', giving a number of names ending in -tot (Yvetot, Criquetot), 'skali' (-écale) and 'dalr', which in Normandy became -dalle. Above all, there are, or have been, nearly 300 places with names formed on Viking personal names. Of these, many are of the hybrid kind where the Viking prefix allies itself with a French suffix, very commonly with the words ville and -bourg. Thus we can find our old acquaintance Toki becoming the eponymous proprietor of Tocqueville, as does Gunni of Gonneville, Kati of Catteville and Kari or Skerri of Cherbourg, to name but a few of this variety. The geographical distribution of Scandinavian personal names is thickest in the two peninsulas which form the Pays de Caux and the northern half of the Cotentin, down the whole length of the river Seine (the main invasion route) and on the lower reaches of the rivers Risle, Dive and Orne. The origins of many Viking personal names have been identified, and as the Dane Worsaae noted as long ago as 1863: 'The old Danish place names of the Danelaw and of the Seineland have the most surprising mutual conformity.' This similarity has led modern scholars to conclude that at least some of the settlers in Normandy must have been Vikings coming over from Britain—a few of them Norwegians, but most of them Danes. The dispersal of 896 was a likely occasion for this movement to have taken place. The analysis of names also showed that, though relatively few, there were enough Norse ones to indicate active relations between Norway and Normandy.

Before the conclusions generally accepted today were arrived at, the question 'whether Normandy was settled by Danes or Norwegians' had been debated for well over a century, one Swedish scholar confusing the issue still further in 1886 by pronouncing that the Normans were not Scandinavian at all! The celebration of the millennium in 1911 gave the debate fresh vigour; but, generally speaking, until the studies of J. Adigard des Gautries and Johannes Steenstrup, Norman scholars were ignorant of nordic languages and names and their Scandinavian colleagues had insufficient acquaintance with Normandy; not until the two sides worked together could the study of Norman place-names make any real headway.

The difficulties experienced by historians evaluating the settlement of Normandy seem to be partly due to the fact that politically, and in their institutions, the Vikings in Normandy moved away from their Scandinavian origins farther and faster than in any of their other western European settlements. This has its parallel in the linguistic field, where it is emphasized by the absence of a native population (such as the Danelaw Angles) speaking dialects similar to the invaders' own. Here, consequently, was no gradual synthesis and mutual enrichment of speech as occurred in England but rather a victory of French over old Norse so thorough and rapid that within a generation or so the latter was having to be learned by Normans as a foreign language! Even their well-known war-cry 'TURAIE' (Thor aid me) was a hybrid word.

Nowhere did the poacher turn gamekeeper more quickly than in Normandy. As Steenstrup puts it: 'Having acquired by rapine considerable goods they formed a new mentality: that of possessors. Henceforth they attached great importance to all measures necessary to protect private property and ensure public peace in which they could securely enjoy it.' Among the sunny orchards of Normandy no egalitarian society of freeholders took root as it was doing under the harsher climate of Danelaw England. Here were no sokemen, no democratic 'thing', no hundred or wapentake courts where all were free to assent or dissent alike.

For the rulers of Normandy were quick to imitate their neighbours in France and Germany and establish themselves as absolute monarchs in the Carolingian tradition. Below the ruler was an aristocracy, but it was one of the large landowners, not of peasantry. The days when the Viking soldiery could cry 'We are all equals' were over, and in Normandy, at least, the age of feudalism had begun.

Chapter V The Eastward Movement

The comparted nature of the Viking movement is indicated by the fact that it has been possible for the last two chapters to be written with scarcely a mention of Sweden or eastern Europe and that during the course of the present one hardly any reference will be necessary to any point on the map west of longitude 15°.

So little do the 'movement west' and the concurrent 'movement east' seem to interrelate that it is hard not to feel that the activities of the Swedes in Russia and the exploits of their Dano-Norwegian contemporaries in the west are purely coincidental. But, however disparate on the surface, the two peaks do spring from a land-mass common to both, with shared historical traditions, shared language and above all an economic and trading system which extended across, and sustained, the whole Viking world.

On the nature and course of Viking activities on the Atlantic sea-board and islands historians have mostly been in general agreement, always bearing in mind that the western Vikings' apparent preoccupation with war and plunder rather than with trade may be due to the one-sided nature of our sources of information. With the coming of better knowledge and mutual understanding such questions as why the Norwegians settled Normandy have now reached a reasonable synthesis!

The same cannot however be said of the Vikings in eastern Europe. Over many recent decades their history from the ninth to the eleventh centuries and the part they played in the foundation of the earliest Russian state have been the subject of an enormous amount of discussion between scholars supporting the 'Normanist' (pro-Scandinavian) and 'anti-Normanist' faction respectively. Even the methods of investigation used by the two sides cannot be agreed on, and since 1917 the dialectic has been further complicated by Marxist views of history on the one side, and contentious statements on the other, like 'northerners must have founded the Russian Kingdom because the indigenous Slavs lacked the necessary empire-building abilities.'

Fortunately, however, for impartial outsiders with neither the time nor inclination to enter this arena, the historical and linguistic evidence has produced certain facts whose truth is beyond reasonable doubt. The first is that the natural direction for the Swedish heartlands to look for expansion and trade is not westwards into the Scandinavian peninsula but eastwards across the Baltic. Opposite Uppland nature has placed first the Åland islands and further east, scattered over the channel, an archipelago called 'The Skift'. The two together provided stepping stones across this neck of the Baltic. Both the archaeological and later the historical evidence make it certain that from pre-Viking times the Swedes and their allies the Gotlanders had established settlements further down the coast, in Estonia, Latvia and Lithuania, and that by the beginning of the ninth century they were penetrating eastward into the continent along both shores of the Gulf of Finland into lake Ladoga and up rivers like the Luga, Pljussa and Dvina.

The Rus

It seems fairly certain that these first northerners ventured into the vast expanses of forest and steppe not as individuals but as members of organized brotherhoods or sodalities, the members of which were pledged on oath to uphold one another's safety and well being. The word in old Norse for these plighted brothers was *Væringjar*, written in Greek *Βάραγγοί* and anglicized as Varangians. (But some scholars think it may simply be a Greek nick-name meaning 'the hoarse ones'—shades of their singing at Hedeby!)

As to the origins of the name Russia there is little doubt that in its earlier form *Rossiya* it derived from the people known as *Rus* or *Ros* (written in Byzantine Greek *'Pως* or *'Pῶσοι*) a name first met with in the 9th century and whose oldest known written occurrence is in the Frankish Annals of 839. Though the word is thought to come from the name *Ruotsi* 'the rowing road' which the Finns called Sweden, it was perhaps in turn connected with Old Norse *Rothsmenn*—the rowers or shipmen. Incidental evidence is always the most convincing: such is the casual remark in 968 of Liudprand, bishop of Cremona, that he had met men known as Rus and that they were the same people otherwise called Northmen; or the Byzantine delegation of 839 to the court of Louis the Pious, two of whom were not Greeks but men who said they were called Rhos and served under a prince with the title Chagan. Moreover, they were found on investigation by the suspicious Franks to be men of *Swedish* origins. These two entirely independent uses of the word *Rus* and its identification with Swede or Northman are backed up by the fact that it was also regularly used by Arab travellers and traders to distinguish people of Scandinavian stock from the rest of the Slav inhabitants of this vast region.

In time the use of this name Rus would spread from the Swedish Viking merchants, traders and warriors and be applied to the non-Scandinavian tribes who became subject to them—some of them, in Esthonia and round lake Ladoga, of Finnish race, the rest Slavs. The Viking Swedes did not, of course, subdue more than a tiny part of the races they encountered. In the south, to east and west respectively, were two great powers of this time: the Arab caliphate of Baghdad and the imperial court of Byzantium (Constantinople). North of the Black Sea, extending from the Caspian to the Crimea were the vast territories of the Khazars and west of them the Bulgars.

All these were powerful peoples, occasionally raided but never seriously threatened by the Rus. But northward again in the upper valleys and tributaries of the Dnieper and Don were many smaller disunited Slav tribes who presented no obstacle to the Vikings' southward progress down the rivers of their region and who no doubt helped to fill up the numbers of many a consignment of slaves.

The earliest historical account dealing with this part of the world is the much-quoted *Russian Primary Chronicle*, traditionally attributed to a Kiev monk named Nestor. This tells how, around the mid-ninth century the Varangians from beyond the sea imposed tribute on various Slav tribes and how one of them, Rurik, was subsequently invited by these tribes to bring his kinsfolk and govern their country. 'These particular Varangians', says the Chronicle, 'were called Rus, as others are called Svie, others Normane, others Angliane, others Gote.' All these names (the 'Anglians' could be Danes from Angeln) sound very convincing, but the difficulty is that the oldest extant manuscripts of the Primary Chronicle date from around 1400, over 500 years later than the events they purport to describe, and so long a tradition may not be reliable. This fact has been seized on by the 'Anti-Normanists' and exhaustive contrary interpretations have been based on it.

Nevertheless, the Chronicle's account of how Rurik fixed his government in 862 at Novgorod, and how two other Rus called Askold and Dir sailed southward down the Dnieper and established themselves at Kiev cannot simply be dismissed in favour of pan-Slavic explanations. Once again the names are remarkably convincing. Rorik and Hoskuld are names (we have already met them) common in the Scandinavian world and so was Dyri; for a Greek scribe to have invented them out of the blue is against all the odds. Moreover, the Vikings on their side bestowed Scandinavian names on both the towns, which remained closely connected with each other down to 997: Kiev was Kœnugarthr, perhaps 'boat town', Novgorod was Holmgarthr 'island town', built on terraces above the river Volkhov. Names are not usually bestowed on places by foreigners without some kind of lasting and significant association between them.

Novgorod's name means 'the new town' in contra-distinction to the Scandinavian Aldeigjuborg, 'old town', which stood near the other end of the river Volkhov eight miles before it flows into lake Ladoga, the present Russian town being called Old (Staraja) Ladoga.

Sweden's merchants and adventurers went east. They had first crossed the Baltic via Gotland to the Latvian coast (above) where a town called Grobin grew up round an early military encampment and as a centre of Gotland trade. They later penetrated the Russian rivers, a network of waterways that, broken by only a few overland portages, led directly to the Black Sea and to the Caspian. The Volkhov, flowing beneath the bluffs of Novgorod (right), and the Dnieper, carried them south to Constantinople; the Volga linked them up with the Baghdad trade.

Archaeological evidence here comes to the support of place-names since this typically placed Viking trading port with access by water straight to Sweden has yielded two unquestionably Scandinavian runic inscriptions of the ninth century and remains of Finnish or Swedish type log-houses. The racial affinities of Aldeigjuborg, whether Slav, Finnish or Swedish, may be better known if a burial ground is found, but meanwhile the completely Slav character of the town is insisted on by Russian archaeologists.

However, though this may be correct for the later excavation levels, no amount of chauvinist history-making can render it entirely so for the earlier ones. Nor, at the other extreme, are the claims of Normanist scholars that the whole town was a Viking colony likely to be any more correct. The truth seems to be that the populations of these trading towns and of the other ones in the Dnieper region associated with the Swedish Vikings probably did remain basically Slav, with the Viking warriors and merchants forming, at least during the first centuries, a fairly numerous dominant class and bringing with them a more advanced material culture.

Trade, and their own enrichment, were the primary concerns of the Scandinavians in Russia, not, as in England or Normandy, the conquest or settlement of the countryside, still less the tilling of the soil. The Arab observer, Ibn Rustah, writing in the 920s, bears this out when he reports that the Rus merchants even after many decades of activity still had no cultivated land but depended for their living on what they could obtain from the land of the Slavs.

In other words their relationship remained a parasitic one and, except in the Finnish area near the Baltic and along the Volkhov river, did not lead to the kind of assimilation with the native population which occurred so rapidly in other countries where the racial stock and language were similar to the Vikings' own. Once the Rus infiltration ended, the whole episode became a thing of the past and correspondingly difficult to explore and evaluate. This is one reason why the story of the 'movement east' has been so fraught with doubts and controversies.

To Byzantium

The twin lodestars on which the Vikings' attention was fixed and which drew them the enormous distances from their Baltic bridgeheads down the rivers and inland seas of eastern Europe were the Arab capital of Baghdad and the Greek capital of Byzantium. It is a measure of Viking merchants' fascination with these exotic civilizations and of their greed for gain that they were able to contemplate and carry out these formidable journeys. From lake Ladoga to Baghdad is 1,900 miles and to Constantinople well over 1,300 miles but these are mere straight lines on a map and give no idea of the real distances to be covered, still less of the endurance required to contend with them year after year and decade after decade.

With an eye on the map let us try and gain some idea of the difficulties and effort involved on one of these journeys. We shall then be able to appreciate better the comment made by the emperor Constantine, about 950, that 'the life of the Rus is a hard one'.

The fortified town of Aldeigjuborg was the northernmost starting point. Here a merchant could rest (if he came from Sweden he had already voyaged 800 miles), tranship his goods, and decide which of the two great Scandinavian routes to the east he would be taking: the Volga route leading south-eastward to the Caspian sea and eventually to Baghdad, or the Dnieper route whose general line was due south and destination Constantinople.

The first step on this latter journey was along the river Volkhov which connects lakes Ladoga and Ilmen, through lands where (if anywhere in Russia) Scandinavian emigrants may have settled alongside those of the Finnish race. On bluffs each side of the Volkhov, just before it reached lake Ilmen, was Novgorod, controlled by the Rus since (if the Primary Chronicle is correct) 862. For those merchants not coming from Sweden, Novgorod rather then Aldeigjuborg would be the rallying point. It is tempting to see in Novgorod's later development as a merchant republic of a rather Venetian type the democratic legacy of its Scandinavian founders. In the event it was the absolutism of the Moscow rulers that set the Russian pattern not the republican spirit of Novgorod.

The next stage of the journey was across lake Ilmen and up the short rivers Lovat, Usivat, and Kasplja, all flowing in a great area of marsh. Then comes one of the sections requiring special effort, a portage across to the banks of the Ilmen just west of the modern town of Smolensk. At this point, called Gnezdevo, a final option for the Volga route was still possible since by following the Dnieper and its tributaries eastward into the hills, a portage could be made to the headwaters of the Oka, a tributary of the Volga. The importance of Gnezdevo as a Dnieper junction and terminus is indicated by the thousands of graves of this period found there. When some of these were excavated by Swedish archaeologists before 1914 the number of objects (including 24 characteristic oval brooches) showing undoubted Scandinavian influence permitted an interpretation strongly in favour of Rus control of the area—an interpretation endorsed by Russian archaeologists of that time. However, the graves excavated after 1917 tell a very different story: out of 700 only two 'were undoubtedly burials of Norsemen'.

At this point west of Smolensk the merchants who had come down from Ladoga might be joined by those taking a short cut from the Baltic (Gulf of Riga) by rowing up the river Dvina; indeed it is the Dvina which the Primary Chronicle calls 'the route to the Varangians', and the Gota Saga tells us that this was the river particularly used by the Gotlanders.

Back on the Dnieper there now began the long river journey (over 300 miles) down the river to Kiev. Here the Dnieper was normally about half a mile across, widening several miles during the spring floods in April and May. Kiev is referred to by the Primary Chronicle as 'the capital of the Varangians' and though no archaeological evidence has survived from earlier than the tenth century it must have been an important gathering place for the Rus merchants from the middle of the ninth. Kiev was the place where the river Dnieper began to cross the steppes, that belt of treeless plains hundreds of miles wide, and extending away to the east for thousands, over which arrived the caravans from China. At Kiev these caravans transferred their goods for the continuing journey west, across the Ukraine to Krakow, Wroclaw and Prague and thence through Germany to the Rhine. With its position at the crossing point of trade routes, Kiev (which was certainly at times under Viking rule) became 'the mother of Russian cities' and the centre of the Russian state.

Though by no means purely a Scandinavian town, Kiev during the ninth and tenth centuries must have been the semi-permanent headquarters of a great many warrior-merchants of Swedish ancestry. In his instruction manual *On the Administration of the Empire* the emperor Constantine tells us: 'At the beginning of November the Rus and all their chieftains leave Kiev and go out on *poliudie* which means their rounds, to the various Slav tribes who pay them tribute. There they are maintained until the departure of the ice in April when they return to Kiev.' It is a fair indication of the parasitic nature of our 'eastern movement' Scandinavians that they billeted themselves on the very people from whom they were exacting tribute. Besides hard cash, much of this tribute will have been in the form of furs (especially sables) and slaves (particularly girls) and this region was the last from which the Viking merchants could gather such merchandise since south of Kiev the steppes were still controlled by the powerful Bulgars and Khazars.

From April to June the merchants remained in Kiev; by June the Dnieper was navigable after the spring floods and the boats moved off in convoy down the river. The emperor Constantine gives a very full account of the hazards encountered by the Rus on the Dnieper between Kiev and the Black Sea. Though they had control of the river itself they had to face attacks from the hostile Khazar tribesmen if ever they required to land, and this need coincided with the most dangerous stretch of the Dnieper, where for forty miles the river runs through granite gorges down a series of cataracts. In his handbook on the Empire, the emperor Constantine gives the names of seven of these Dnieper rapids and whirlpools both in their Slav and their 'Russian' forms, and, although the names are a little difficult to translate (three of them end in *fors* 'waterfall'), there is no doubt about their Norse origin. It is a very useful piece of independent evidence and one irrefutable by the anti-Normanists that in the mid-tenth century 'Russian' was clearly a Nordic tongue. Further name-evidence, this time of men's names, is provided by the Primary Chronicle which lists fourteen recognizably Scandinavian witnesses to a treaty of 912 between the Greek emperors and Oleg 'great prince of the Rus'. Their names, as might be expected, are mainly east Swedish or perhaps Finnish—at any rate not one of them is Slavonic.

Having got through the rapids (they are near the modern town of Dnepropetrovsk) by poling, wading and portage our Rus merchants next had to negotiate shallows and sandbars until—six weeks after leaving Kiev—the Dnieper delta was reached. Among the channels of the river as it made its way into the Black Sea was an island called Berezanji, where the easternmost of all known runic inscriptions has been found—a memorial stone cut by Grani to his comrade Karli, and sure proof that the Northmen reached these parts.

Constantine tells us that, about this stage of the journey, the Rus merchants would offer up sacrifices to prosper their trade. One of these occasions (though it is on the Volga, not the Dnieper) has been graphically described by an Arab trader called Ahmad Ibn Fadhlan. He was writing in 921 when the Scandinavians in this part of the world still seem to have been entirely pagan. 'When the merchants came to this anchorage they all left the boats, carrying ashore with them bread, meat, onions, milk and *nabid* [an alcoholic drink]. They go to a high wooden pillar with a human face, round which were smaller figures, and behind them tall posts in the ground. Each merchant approaches the tall figure, prostrates himself before it and says "Oh Lord I have come a long way and I have with me this many slave-girls and that many sable furs [he mentions whatever merchandise he has with him]. Now I come to you with this offering—and he places what he has with him before the high wooden figure—Please send me a merchant who has lots of dinars and dirhems [Arabic coinage] who will buy from me on my terms and without too much bartering".' Ibn Fadhlan describes how the Rus reward their gods after successful trading by slaughtering sheep or cattle and throwing part of the meat to the tall figure and the smaller figures around— the heads are hung on the posts. After nightfall of course the dogs come and devour the lot, but the trader will say '"Assuredly my Lord is pleased with me and has eaten my offerings".'

No doubt, on the Constantinople journey, the Viking merchants would also invoke the gods for a smooth passage across the Black Sea. This last stage of the journey was over 350 miles straight sailing or much more if the boats hugged its western shoreline. Not for nothing had the Greeks christened this sea *Euxine* 'favourable', hoping thereby to propitiate its sudden and violent storms.

The huge city of Byzantium with perhaps half a million inhabitants and twelve miles of fortifications would be quite unlike anything our Swedish warrior-merchants had ever seen—indeed there was no other place in the western world to match it for size and civilization, and most important from their point of view as a trading centre and emporium. Such a city was proof

Two powerful tribes with whom the Rus, the Swedish Vikings in the East, were obliged to share control of trade in Russia were the Khazars, based at Itil on the Caspian, and the Bulgars, whose eastern centre at Bulgar commanded the Volga bend. Conflict was inevitable, coming to a head for instance when a Viking attack on Constantinople first involved annexing the lands of the western Bulgars, or when, defeated by the Byzantine Empire, the Rus were obliged by a peace treaty with the Greeks to make war on the Bulgars on their behalf (above).

against any force the Vikings could bring against it, used as they were to getting their own way over most of the world. They had made attempts from time to time—one of the earliest was led by Hoskuld and Dyri from Kiev in the 860s and another by Rurik's descendant Oleg about 907, which secured the 912 treaty. From then, except for two more unsuccessful attacks by Igor in 941 and 944, there was peace, and a further treaty was signed between the Greeks and the Rus in 945. 967-8 saw the decisive showdown between the kingom of Kiev-Novgorod and the empire of Byzantium. In 967 Svyatoslav virtually annexed western Bulgaria, set up a capital (Svetlav) on the Danube delta and from there threatened Constantinople. Next year, however, he was besieged by the emperor and the Rus suffered a humiliating defeat; but this in no way affected their privileged trading status.

The ships and seamanship of the Byzantine navy were in themselves probably not the Vikings' equal but they were able to repel them on several occasions by employing their secret weapon. This was 'Greek Fire', thought to be a crude petroleum ignited under pressure and hurled against the Viking ships, and it was entirely successful in repelling the final Russian attack under Vladimir in 1043.

In comparison with the mighty Byzantine empire the Vikings were relatively weak, and few in numbers. Far from home and the possibility of reinforcements, strangers in a hostile land, their lines of supply and communication unduly long, the Vikings' powers of persuasion were nevertheless able to secure by these treaties terms which were comparable with those enjoyed by their contemporaries in their much stronger position in the English Danelaw. True they were not allowed to carry weapons while in Mikligarth (Constantinople), they must return to Kiev every autumn, they could not buy more than a certain ration of silk (which must be stamped by the customs); but on the other hand the treaties secured their legal rights and personal wergild not to mention certain other tangible benefits like free victualling for a month, provisions and equipment for their return journey, and even (perhaps) free baths!

Although the collective wisdom of *Völuspá* or *Hávamál* do not reveal the actual words 'If you can't beat them join them' it is a piece of advice completely in line with Viking pragmatism and the tradition of selling one's sword arm to the highest bidder. Since they certainly could not beat them, those of the Scandinavian adventurers who were more inclined by temperament to war than to trade had from earliest times been taking service with the Greek emperors. Large numbers of them gave up trade and joined the imperial army, serving over a wide field, from Mesopotamia in the east to Italy and Crete in the west. Towards the end of the tenth century the reputation of these Scandinavian mercenaries was such that from their number an *élite* corps was chosen to act as the emperor's personal bodyguard. Between about 980 and 1070 this Varangian Guard became a kind of Foreign Legion attracting young men not only from among the

Swedish Vikings but from all over the Scandinavian world. One of the best known of these was Harald 'Hardradi' Sigurdsson, half-brother of St. Olaf of Norway. Aged 15, Harald escaped from Norway after Olaf's defeat and death at Stiklestad (1030) and made his way to Russia which was then ruled over by Yaroslav, one of the most distinguished rulers of the Novgorod-Kiev kingdom, and the last of them to maintain close contacts between Sweden and Russia. After service with Yaroslav (whose daughter he married) Harald sailed to Constantinople in 1034 with a retinue of 500 'valiant soldiers' and for the next ten years served in the Varangian Guard in campaigns all over the Mediterranean region. Unusually for a Viking warrior, the highly-coloured exploits attributed to him in Harald's Saga can be checked against a contemporary Greek source which describes him as 'Araltes son to the King of Varangia' (Norway and Sweden were all one to the Greeks) and says that one Emperor made him *spatharokandates* or troop leader, while another refused him permission to return to Norway. When he did leave it was by stealth and by the way he had originally come—Kiev, Novgorod and Aldeigjuborg.

Thus the word 'Varangian', which had originally meant a brotherhood of merchants, now signified a particular kind of Viking warrior: the change of meaning is part and parcel of the dual nature of these eastern Vikings. After 1066 the composition of the Varangian Guard was altered by the arrival of a large number of Englishmen, perhaps mainly from the Danelaw, who could not stomach the tyranny of Norman William. From now on, the Guard, which survived for a further 150 years, was more English than Viking in composition.

By the late tenth and early eleventh centuries the Rus kingdom too was changing; as its ties with the Byzantine empire increased so those with Scandinavia were loosening. In 988 the Rus leader Vladimir, father of the still more celebrated Yaroslav, decided to make the Christianity of the Greek church the official religion of the Kiev-Novgorod state, and from then until his death in 1015 he proceeded to build many churches and to baptize his subjects in the Dnieper. This was at a time when the Swedish homeland was still mainly pagan. Furthermore the language of the new Russian state was by now no longer Scandinavian but was becoming Slavonic, though using the Greek alphabet.

Despite the fact that Vladimir was later canonized and though his wife Anna was the emperor Basil's sister he seems in some matters to have carried on much as his grandfather Igor had done in the days when Ahmad Ibn Fadhlan described the scene at the Kiev-Novgorod court: 'It is customary for the king of the Rus to have a bodyguard in his castle of 400 reliable men willing to die for him. Each of these has a slave-girl to wait on him, wash him, and serve him, and another to sleep with. These 400 sit below the royal throne: a large and bejewelled platform which also accommodates the forty slave-girls of his harem. The King frequently has public intercourse with one of these. He does not bother leaving his throne when he wants to make water, he has a basin brought to him for the purpose; and when he wants to go riding his horse is brought right up to the throne. He has a deputy to lead his armies in battle, fight his enemies, and hold audiences with his subjects.'

As for the towns of the Rus, their creation or enlargement as vigorous trading centres, from Ladoga in the north to Kiev in the south and from Polotsk on the Dvina over to Rostov in the east, was , even more than the mixing of the Scandinavian and the Slav races, the Vikings' truly significant contribution to the mighty land of Russia.

To Baghdad

We have followed the Rus merchants south down the Dnieper route and across the Black Sea to their goal at Constantinople, and have looked at some of the lasting relationships formed by them with the Byzantine world. We now accompany their fellow Vikings down the Volga trail to the southeast, destination Baghdad, with staging points at Bulgar on the Volga bend, and Gurgan.

This was a much longer and still more arduous journey, with an Arab city at the end of it where the status of the Rus was that of barbarian traders and not, as in Constantinople, subjects also of a respected neighbouring power. We may be sure that, at the one level, no Rus was ever offered the command of the Caliph's bodyguard nor the hand of his sister in marriage, nor, at the other, did the Baghdad welcome include hot baths and free provisions for weary Viking merchants.

This trading journey would begin along the little rivers eastward from lake Ladoga and portages were necessary before the Volga could be reached. In this region, and in those of Jaroslav and Vladimir further west, between the Volga and the Oka a number of graves have been found with Scandinavian objects in them indicating that there may have been a few small communities of Norsemen; but on the Volga route there were no opportunities for setting up or taking over permanent towns as there had been on the Dnieper. 'When they have come from their land and anchored on, or tied up at the shore of, the Volga, which is a great river, they build big houses of wood on the shore, each holding ten to twenty persons more or less.'

At the Volga bend, where the great river turns sharply south, lay the town of Bulgar, the chief settlement and trading-post of the eastern section of the tribe of that name. Near Bulgar the river Kama joins the Volga, and down it came trappers, some Rus, others native, bringing furs from the endless forests of Siberia to the north-east—highly prized sables, marten and ermine, fox, squirrel and beaver. These, many of them extorted as tribute by the Rus, would all add their odorous complement to the other Viking merchandise—amber, hides, honey, swords and slaves. At Bulgar the Rus would meet for the first time the camel trains coming from Tashkent, Samarkand and Bokhara. It is to the Arabs, some of them the owners of these caravan trains, that we are indebted for so many obviously eye-witness, if sometimes biased, accounts of the eastern Rus. More literate and sophisticated than the Norsemen, the Arabs were clearly fascinated by these 'big men, all of them red-haired, with white bodies'.

Much of the eastern silver that found its way back to Scandinavia will have been received at Bulgar from Muslim traders in exchange for the products collected by the Vikings in northern lands. For it was not Greek but Arabian 'Cufic' silver from a number of mints from Mesopotamia to Samarkand that found its way back to Scandinavia (especially Birka); and it was along the Volga, not the Dnieper, that this silver current seems to have flowed, at least until about 880.

After Bulgar began what must have seemed the never-ending course of the Volga down the steppes, passing the point where the river Don is within reach and finally reaching the Volga delta on the Caspian Sea where stood the Khazar capital of Itil or Atil. The Norsemen's attitude to the powerful Khazars would be a respectful one; the Khazars levied customs duties on the Don and on the Volga and could prevent the Rus using the rivers if they so wished.

Important caravan routes from Bokhara and further east crossed the Volga on their way west to Kiev and on to western Europe and at this point, as at Bulgar, the Viking traders would be able to exchange their northern merchandise either for goods more acceptable in the markets of Gurgan and Baghdad or else for Cufic coinage to take back with them when they next returned to Gotland or Sweden.

The presence of this silver in Scandinavia was one of the factors which stimulated internal trade (and piracy) there during the early part of the Viking period; and when this supply of Cufic coinage dried up it was replaced by silver (probably originating in the Harz mountains) looted or exacted from England and her neighbours.

Itil at the north-west end of the Caspian Sea and Gurgan at the south-east will have provided further trading opportunities for the less easily satisfied or more adventurous of the Rus traders. Another Arab writer, after listing their merchandise, tells us: 'Sometimes they bring their wares by camel from Gurgan to Baghdad where Slavonic eunuchs interpret for them'—these latter no doubt themselves the unfortunate victims of earlier Viking slave raids. For such inveterate wet-bobs as the Vikings to leave their boats and become camel-drivers or muleteers on a 700-mile trek across the Persian mountains indicates how powerful was the lure of Baghdad and its riches; not least the fact that in the Caliphate a slave would fetch a much-enhanced price—between 100 and 600 dirhems.

If our knowledge of the Viking 'movement east' depended purely on archaeological evidence and included no written accounts, it would be

Traffic in silver was the basis of trade with Russia, especially in coinage from the Caliphate of Baghdad. But Rus/Bulgar warring finally threatened the Volga route, and the supply from the East was diminishing anyway after the end of the 10th century. Scandinavia then turned to England and Germany and to the western Caliphate for silver.

scanty indeed and almost non-existent eastwards of the upper Volga, where the few graves already referred to may represent accidental deaths on trading trips. Deaths on these long voyages and in these arduous conditions there must have been—perhaps as often the result of illness and disease as from wounds received in battle. The funeral customs of these Swedish Vikings (already mingled with Slav practices) obviously made an impression on their Arab observers. The following account of a Rus cremation on the Volga was written by Ahmad Ibn Fadhlan when serving on an embassy from Baghdad to the Bulgars 921–2: 'They burn him in this fashion: they leave him for the first ten days in a grave. His possessions they divide into three parts: one part for his daughters and wives; another for garments to clothe the corpse; another part covers the cost of the intoxicating drink which they consume in the course of ten days, uniting sexually with women and playing musical instruments. Meanwhile, the slave-girl who gives herself to be burned with him, in these ten days drinks and indulges in pleasure; she decks her head and her person with all sorts of ornaments and fine dress and so arrayed gives herself to the men. The ninth day, having drawn the ship up on to the river bank, they guarded it. In the middle of the ship they prepared a dome of wood and covered this with various sorts of fabrics. Then they brought a couch and put it on the ship and covered it with a mattress of Greek brocade. Then came an old woman whom they call the Angel of Death, and she spread upon the couch the furnishing mentioned. It is she who has charge of the clothes-making and arranging all things, and it is she who kills the girl slave. I saw that she was a strapping old woman, fat and louring. The tenth day, they brought the deceased out of the ground and put him inside the pavilion and put around him different kinds of flowers and fragrant plants. Many men and women gathered and played musical instruments and each of his kinsmen built a pavilion around his pavilion at some distance. The slave-girl arrayed herself and went to the pavilions of the kinsmen of the dead man, and the master of each had sexual intercourse once with her, saying in a loud voice, "Tell your master that I have done the duty (or exercised the right) of love and friendship". And so, as she went to all the pavilions to the last one, all the men had intercourse with her. When this was over, they cut a dog in two halves and put it into the boat, then, having cut the head off a rooster, they threw it, head and body to the right and left of the ship. After that the group of men who have cohabited with the slave-girl make of their hands a sort of paved way whereby the girl, placing her feet on the palms of the men, comes down and mounts again to the ship and recites many things. She goes into the pavilion in which her husband has been put, and six of the relatives of her husband go into the pavilion and unite sexually with this wife in the presence of the dead man. When they have finished these duties of love, the old woman who, according to the belief of these people, is the Angel of Death arrives and lays the wife to sleep beside her husband. Of the six men, two seize the legs of the

Among other ways of celebrating a ship-burial was the custom of outlining the shape of a boat in stones over the place of cremation. A Rus cremation on the Volga was marked by a mound topped with an inscribed post.

slave-girl, and two others her hands, and the old woman, twisting her veil, puts it around her neck and gives the ends to the two other men so that they can pull it so tight that the soul escapes from her body. Then the closest relative of the dead man, after they had placed the girl whom they have killed beside her master, came, took a piece of wood which he lighted at a fire, and walked backwards with his head toward the boat and his face turned (towards the people), with one hand holding the kindled stick and the other covering his anus, being completely naked, for the purpose of setting fire to the wood that had been made ready beneath the ship. Then the people came up with tinder and other firewood, each holding a piece of wood of which he had set fire to an end and which he put into the pile of wood beneath the ship. Thereupon the flames engulfed the wood, then the ship, the pavilion, the man, the girl, and everything in the ship. A powerful, fearful wind began to blow so that the flames became fiercer and more intense. And actually an hour had not passed before the ship, the wood, the girl and her master were nothing but cinders and ashes.

'Then they constructed in the place where had been the ship which they had drawn up out of the river something like a small round hill, in the middle of which they erected a great post of birch wood, on which they wrote the name of the man and the name of the Rus king and they departed.'

A wooden post soon rots, and a consuming fire leaves little evidence after a thousand years; but the Vikings practised burial as well as cremation and to a certain extent Ibn Fadhlan's account is borne out by the archaeological evidence from graves elsewhere in Russia. In the Dnieper burial grounds the fact that the women's body in the man's grave never wears a Scandinavian-type brooch implies that the victim was usually a native slave girl or concubine, and Ibn Rustah, another Arab writer, says of a Rus leader's burial 'they also put his favourite "wife" in the grave with him, while she is still living. And so the entrance to the grave is stopped, and she dies there.'

These pagan ceremonies on the banks of gloomy Russian rivers have the effect of removing these eastern, partly Slav, Vikings even further from our ken and from that of their own western contemporaries than the thousand years of time and two thousand miles of space which actually separate them.

And, although there is evidence from Birka, Oseberg and even from Iceland, of burials accompanied by ritual murder, it is hard to imagine either that, or suttee, or ritual intercourse being the regular practice, even in those pagan days, in the Scandinavian homelands; still less among the hardworking, hard-headed settlers in the English Danelaw, towards whom, with some relief, we may now retrace our westward steps.

Chapter VI   The Empire of Knut

The second Scandinavian campaign against Britain

The expulsion in 954 of Eirik Bloodaxe from the York kingdom of Northumbria ended the first era of Viking enterprise against England, and before the next waves of Scandinavian attack broke on her shores a relatively peaceful quarter-century intervened. All this time the transmutation of Danes and Norwegians into Englishmen was continuing—this process of assimilation being undoubtedly helped on by the policy of firmness, combined with generosity, adopted by the rulers of Wessex, from Alfred the Great onwards, towards their Scandinavian subjects, at any rate up to the reign of his great grandson Edgar, who became king (aged 16) in 959 and reigned till 975. He was the king who, tradition states, was rowed on the river Dee by six subject princes and was, according to his obituary, 'Honoured throughout many nations, far and wide over the gannet's bath'—no doubt a way of describing the seas around the British Isles.

Edgar's legislation for the Danelaw (as it was now becoming known) recognized the right of its Danish inhabitants to their own legal and social customs. 'It is my will that there should be in force among the Danes such good law as they best decide on; and I have ever allowed them this . . . because of your loyalty which you have always shown me', states Edgar's Decree of 962. This degree of autonomy and freedom from royal interference is probably one of the reasons why the Danes both in England and in their homeland conducted themselves tranquilly during the reign of 'Edgar the Peaceful'. The raiding had ceased; but there is good reason to suppose that all through the tenth century the steady, and on the whole peaceable, flow of settlers from the Scandinavian world into the Danelaw was continuing apace so long as productive land remained to be taken up.

Now and again the names of immigrants emerge from the general anonymity: Kormak's Saga records how in 967 Kormak and his brother

Thorgils founded settlements on the Yorkshire coast. Thorgils (his nickname was Skarthi—'hare-lipped') gave his name to Scarborough, while Kormak, with the by-name Fleinn ('the sharp-tongued person' or 'the arrow') almost certainly founded Flamborough, sixteen miles to the south and to this day called by its inhabitants 'Fleinbro'.

King Edgar died suddenly in July, 975. The harmonious state of affairs described by his obituarist did not long survive his death. Both Edgar's sons—stepbrothers—were minors. The elder, Edward (later Saint Edward), was murdered in less than three years and the younger one came to the throne under a cloud of suspicion that was to deprave his character, overshadow his long reign (978–1016), destroy the prestige of the English crown and make the name of Aethelred the Redeless—'Ethelred the Unready'—a by-word for centuries to come.

The news that a strong and able king had been replaced by a boy of eleven will soon have crossed the 'gannet's bath', so it is no surprise to find the Anglo-Saxon Chronicle for 980 recording the ravaging of Southampton and of Cheshire by pirate hosts. During the decade that follows, England's continuing weakness and relative disorganization invited further Viking attacks, and it is again no surprise that these were all aimed at Saxon England and never, at this juncture, against cousins in the Danelaw. Whether these Anglo-Danes and Anglo-Norwegians of the Danelaw took any active steps actually to aid and abet the raiders we do not know; certainly their kith and kin in Normandy were doing so by making their harbours available to the pirates, until in 991 Ethelred and duke Richard agreed by treaty not to shelter each other's enemies.

These raids during the decade 981–91 seem to have been individually organized expeditions undertaken for the original Viking purpose of plunder—treasure and prisoners—and not with any thought of settlement. Probably many of those taking part were Jomsvikings from the Baltic. But they differed from the raids of the ninth century in one important factor: their leaders now included scions of the ruling houses of Denmark and Norway and what began as private freebootery was to alter, before the year 1000, into a campaign conducted on a royal and national footing. Two of these leaders were the young Svein, later called 'Forkbeard', son of king Harald Gormsson of Denmark, and his Norwegian brother-in-law Olaf Tryggvason who later both became kings of their respective countries.

Heimskringla tells us that Olaf harried far and wide in the land, over a period of four years, ending up in the Scilly Isles. In 991 the Anglo-Saxon Chronicle takes up the story, and records his harrying of the Kentish coast 'and thence to Ipswich, overrunning all the countryside and so on to Maldon' in Essex where he defeated the local ealdorman and his thegns. Olaf was afterwards baptized and, says *Heimskringla*, 'now he went about peacefully, for England was a Christian country and he was also a Christian.'

Cynics may regard Olaf's conversion as yet another example of Viking opportunism; certainly the treaty concluded later in the year with Aethelred brought him and his followers enormous rewards. Its clauses included an amnesty on all past hostilities and one protecting English and Scandinavian merchant shipping, but its most significant statement was that £22,000 in gold and silver had been given to the raiders as the price of peace—though the versions of the Anglo-Saxon Chronicle only admit to a £10,000 payment.

Whatever the sum involved, this policy of buying off the invaders would prove ruinous for England during the next quarter-century. Had Aethelred used the respite from attack thus purchased to set the country's defences in order this 'Danegeld'—the first English payment since 865—might have proved money well-spent. But since he did not, and since the rest of his reign is a story of indecision, treachery and general mismanagement, this payment of 991 merely set a disastrous precedent.

In any case, it was Aethelred himself, who, a year later, broke the treaty in an attempt to take the Norse fleet by surprise, and from then on hostilities once again became continuous. In 993 the Chronicle records attacks on Anglian Northumbria and also, for the first time, on the shores of the Danelaw itself, when 'the host came to the mouth of the Humber and did much damage there, both in Lindsey and in [Viking] Northumbria'. This must be taken to indicate that by now the Danelaw descendants of the earlier Norsemen were no longer regarded as compatriots by these latter-day Vikings, but simply as inhabitants of an enemy nation. The attacks on England were in fact coming to resemble warfare on a national footing. As Professor Jones puts it: 'The pattern of *viking* was changing when great kings and kings-to-be, rather than the old-style captains brought their wave-stallions over the ocean's back to England.'

In September, 994, the two royal leaders arrived in company: Olaf Tryggvason of Norway, and Svein, now king of Denmark, sailed up the Thames with a large fleet (the Chronicle says 94 ships) and began a continuous attack on London. Failing to capture or burn the town, the Vikings wreaked their vengeance on the south-eastern counties and quite in the old style 'got themselves horses, rode far and wide wherever they pleased, and continued to do unspeakable damage'. The upshot of this was a cash payment by Aethelred of £16,000 and winter quarters for the host at Southampton with free provisioning from the kingdom of Wessex. Once again the Chronicle records Olaf's confirmation and king Aethelred's sponsorship—perhaps the occasion in 991 had been simply a *primsigning*? More important, from the English point of view, was Olaf's undertaking—which he kept—to leave the country. After his departure in 995, accompanied by an English-born bishop and priests, his future career lay in the Baltic lands, where this Viking warrior and breaker of heathen sanctuaries completed the conversion of Norway begun by his great grandfather Harald Bluetooth. In the year 1000 Olaf Tryggvason met his death at the sea-battle

The late 10th-century raids on England began as the usual private enterprises but turned into a national campaign when the future kings of Norway and Denmark joined in. They 'got themselves horses' and 'rode far and wide'. Perhaps the fine Viking stirrup found in Gloucestershire (left) was one of theirs. Danish power was growing, a new-found national unity stemming from the mid-10th-century efforts of Gorm, the king who used the name Denmark for the first time in runes on the memorial to his wife that he raised at Jelling (above).

124

of Svold, when Svein acquired not only the Vik but the overlordship of all Norway.

Unlike Olaf, king Svein had made Aethelred no promises, and though we do not hear of his personal presence again in England for ten years there is no doubt that the Danish army, which from 997 onwards systematically raided every part of Wessex, was (though containing mercenaries from all over Scandinavia) essentially a royal force controlled by Svein from Denmark.

Moreover, after 1002 Svein had a standing pretext for attacking England, since in that year Aethelred sent secret instructions throughout the country that on the 13th of November all Danes should be slain 'because he had been told they wished to deprive him of his life by treachery'. Clearly such an order would not have much effect in the Danelaw, where the Danes outnumbered the English; but in Wessex and those parts where they formed a minority the slaughter of Danes must have been considerable.

Aethelred justified the massacre by likening the Danes to 'tares that had sprung up among the wheat'; but, moral considerations apart, the move was a politically inept one, and his relations with Svein were further worsened by the fact that among the victims were the latter's sister Gunnhild, together with her husband and son.

Danish ascendancy

To understand thoroughly the course of this second, and major Scandinavian campaign against England, leading as it did to the country's merger in a North Sea empire, it is necessary to take a closer look at the contemporary Danish scene.

It soon becomes evident that this is one of Denmark's periods of ascendancy over the rest of Scandinavia; a time when this small country was rich enough and secure enough from neighbouring interference for her kings to contemplate the conquest of England not as the result of individual Viking enterprise but as a matter of Danish foreign policy. Indeed, compared with this national initiative, individual Viking enterprise and traditional Viking methods of organization now appear rather ineffective. We may remind ourselves that 1014, the year of the Danish conquest of England, was also the year in which Viking forces signally—and permanently—failed in the not dissimilar enterprise of conquering Ireland. Sigund the Stout, earl of Orkney, and his confederates gathered Vikings to their banners from all parts of western Europe but they were doomed to failure and defeat at the battle of Clontarf (April, 1014) as much as anything because they lacked the unified resources of wealth and organized manpower that the Danish monarchy was able to bring to bear against England.

The beginnings of this Danish ascendancy go back to the time of king Gorm, and it is symbolic of Denmark's new unity that the name of the country DANMARK first appears (c. 950) in native runes on the memorial stone at Jelling which Gorm dedicated to his wife Thyri. Gorm was succeeded by king Harald, who later in his reign (c. 980) saw fit to describe himself on the other memorial stone at Jelling as 'that Harald who won for himself the whole of Denmark and Norway and made the Danes Christian'. Unity makes for strength; for the first time a Danish king could feel that he had no rivals within the country and nothing to fear from the German states to the south. And, however open to question (certainly in the theological sense) was Harald's claim to have 'made the Danes Christian', may we not premise a new accession of energy in a country which had at least begun to throw off the bonds of heathendom and superstition?

In the matter of military organization we are on firmer ground. Four large army camps dating from between the years 970 and 1020 have been discovered in Denmark and since these (there may have been others) were capable of holding far more men than the king's normal bodyguard they are very likely to have been constructed for the specific purpose of accommodating and training troops assembled for the campaign against England, as well as maintaining control over Denmark.

These camps were well dispersed throughout Denmark: two in Jutland, one at Odense (on Funen) and one on the west coast of Zealand. This last, the Trelleborg camp, has been the most thoroughly excavated, and it is thought that the 48 barrack-buildings found there may well have housed a force of over 1,000. Each camp was laid out with a precision and exactitude not equalled since Roman times: their overall planning, the uniformity of their barracks (shaped like inverted boats) and the fact that the four camps could have housed a grand total of at least 4,000 men are all witnesses to the strength and discipline exerted by the Danish monarchy at this period, in the persons of king Harald Bluetooth and king Svein Forkbeard.

In addition to being absolute ruler of a unified Denmark, it is clear that Svein, with the resources at his command, was also in fairly full control of events in the disorganized and disheartened realm of Aethelred the Redeless. Had he so wished he could perhaps have become king of England as early as 994. But as long as this rich country was able to yield tribute it was clearly to Svein's advantage not to kill the goose until the last of the golden eggs had been laid. The sums paid were indeed, by contemporary standards, vast: the £16,000 we noted in 994 had jumped to £24,000 by 1002, £36,000 by 1007 and £48,000 by 1012—these are the figures given by the Anglo-Saxon Chronicle. Then there was the payment of £21,000 apparently made to Svein's general, Thorkell the Tall, in 1014, besides numbers of occasions when counties and lesser communities bought off the attackers with their individual tribute geld. Finally, both versions of the Chronicle record the enormous sum of £72,000 paid by the country to its new king Knut in 1018 'in addition to that which the citizens of London paid, which was eleven thousand pounds'.

Like three other army camps of similar design that have been found in Denmark, Trelleborg dates from the opening of the 11th century when troops were being massed for the invasion of England. Inside a circular rampart (above) the 16 main barrack blocks (one of which has been reconstructed—right and below) could each accommodate about 60 men. The four camps together had a complement of at least 4,000.

It would have been the weather-vanes at the bows of many of the ships of the Danish invasion fleet that caused the chronicler to comment on their 'brazen prows'. One that has survived in Norway (above) shows a row of holes for the pendants that can be seen beneath the vanes someone scratched on a piece of wood found at Bergen (below).

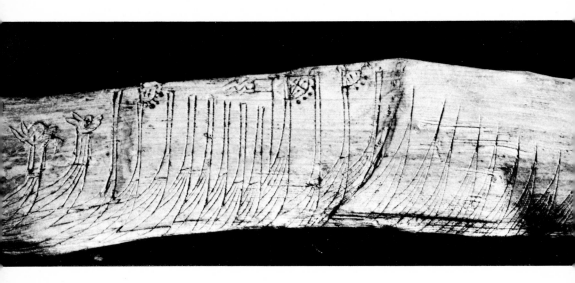

Indeed, throughout Knut's reign, a regular annual army-tax, or 'heregeld' took the place of the lump sum exactions of previous years. Though some of this river of gold and silver flowed into private hands all over the Scandinavian world, by far the greater volume poured into the Danish royal treasury. King Svein had nothing to lose. In the words of Professor Jones: 'To attack the unhappy country was to be paid to go away, and to be paid to go away kept your army in being until you attacked again ... literally, England paid for her conquest with her own money.'

Britain's capitulation

Because they came for booty and tribute the raiders of the period were all the more difficult for the English to deal with. Had these Vikings, many of them perhaps Jomsvikings again, been mainly interested, like those a century earlier, in acquiring land and in becoming settlers they might have been controlled and contained by the boroughs set up in England for just this purpose from Alfred's time onwards. But against these professional soldiers who, because their concern was with loot not land, retained their full mobility the English strongholds were relatively ineffective – in any case many of them may have fallen into disrepair by this time.

Through all the early years of the eleventh century therefore the Chronicle has constantly to tell of an army which 'rode far and wide as it pleased' destroying and burning innumerable manors and any larger place whose citizens were unable to defend it: among the towns which suffered were Norwich, Thetford, Cambridge, Northampton, Oxford, Exeter, Wallingford, Bedford and Canterbury. By 1011, says the Chronicle, the Vikings had overrun East Anglia, Essex, Middlesex, and the counties of Oxford, Cambridge, Hertford, Buckingham, Bedford, Huntingdon (half), Northampton (a great part), Kent, Sussex, Surrey, Berkshire and a great part of Wiltshire. This enumeration makes it clear that with the exception of East Anglia the object of Svein's attack was (like that of the Viking raids of the 870s) essentially the expanded kingdom of Wessex, and not the regions of Anglian settlement.

Two years later, in 1013, 'before the month of August' Svein finally moved in for the kill. A chronicler's description of his fleet, 'with towered ships and brazen prows assembled round the Royal vessel which excelled all the others in beauty', evokes once again the might of the Danish Crown at this period. Svein made his landfall in Kent, but soon moved up the North Sea coast and into the estuary of the Humber. From there he sailed up the tidal river Trent, penetrating into the heart of the Danelaw at Gainsborough. This was an ideal centre at which to receive the apparently free and willing submission of every part of Danish England, as itemized by the Chronicle: 'Then Earl Uhtred and all Northumbria straightway submitted to him, and all the people of Lindsey, and then the people belonging to the Five

Boroughs, and soon afterwards all the Danes to the north of Watling Street; and he was given hostages from every shire.'

It next remained for Svein to secure his recognition by the inhabitants of Saxon England as *de facto* ruler outside the Danelaw and south of Watling Street. Here he was dealing with a very different and, on the whole, inimical populace whose submission was to be achieved by a deliberate display of Viking 'frightfulness'. This ranged over the whole of Wessex as far west as Bath: as the Chronicle tersely put it: 'they did the greatest mischief that any host was capable of'. This campaign of 1013 resulted in the eventual capitulation of London and in the whole nation, with varying degrees of willingness, accepting Svein as their undisputed king. Aethelred and his wife and sons sought refuge in Normandy at the court of his brother-in-law duke Richard.

At this point, however, fate intervened against the Danes. On the 3rd of February, 1014, Svein, first Danish king of England, died suddenly on the road from Gainsborough to Bury St. Edmunds. The Danish forces immediately recognized his son Knut (Canute) as king, and no doubt the Danelaw acclaimed him likewise, but, as was to be expected, the reaction to this news over the rest of England was quite different. The moment they heard that their inveterate foe was removed from the scene the councillors of Wessex sent a deputation to Normandy inviting Aethelred back to England, 'declaring that no lord was dearer to them than their rightful lord (if only he would govern his kingdom more justly than he had done in the past)'. The (not altogether reliable) Saga of the Jomsvikings states that after Svein's death the Londoners also plotted a massacre of the Danish garrisons. This is not mentioned by the Anglo-Saxon Chronicle, but if it occurred it would explain the Danish determination to conquer England once and for all.

Olaf Haraldsson, soon to be king of Norway, chanced to be in a Norman port with some ships, and was no doubt delighted to ferry Aethelred back to England on his Dane-harrying mission. 'He came with levies at full strength into Lindsey before they were prepared and they made raids and burned and slew every human being they could find . . . he gave orders to pay the host that lay at Greenwich £21,000 . . . Eadric betrayed Siferth and Morcar the chief thanes of the Seven Boroughs by enticing them into his chamber, where they were basely done to death. The king then confiscated all their property, and ordered Siferth's widow to be seized. . . .'

Indiscriminate slaughter, danegeld, murder, injustice—it reads like a catalogue of Viking terrorism. But now (so far had Aethelred drifted from the principles of his great forebear, Alfred) the perpetrators were Anglo-Saxons.

Something was indeed rotten, but in the state of England rather than that of Denmark, whence Knut arrived in September, 1015, with a large fleet and the support of his elder brother king Harald Sveinsson. The *Deeds of Knut* (its other title is *The Praise of Emma)* describes the host in splendid

SCOTLAND

Tyne

DURHAM

North Sea

NORTHUMBRIA Tees

IRELAND

YORK Stamford Bridge 1066
TADCASTER Gate Fulford 1066
Ouse

Humber

LINDSEY

GAINSBOROUGH
TORKSEY
LINCOLN

CHESTER

DANELAW

Dee

DERBY NOTTINGHAM

Trent

STAMFORD

LEICESTER

Welland

Ouse

EAST
ANGLIA

NORWICH

THETFORD

NORTHAMPTON
WORCESTER

BURY ST EDMUNDS
CAMBRIDGE
BEDFORD
IPSWICH

WALES

MERCIA

OXFORD

MALDON

WALLINGFORD
LONDON
Ashingdon 1016

BATH

Thames
GREENWICH
CANTERBURY

WESSEX

SOUTHAMPTON

Hastings 1066

EXETER

NORMANDY

*The main towns of Knut's England and the sites of the battles that decided the country's
subsequent life under Norman rule.*

terms: 'in it there was neither slave nor freedman, nor anyone weak with old
age; all were nobles, all vigorous with the strength of complete manhood.'

During that autumn and winter the Danes harried in Wessex and the
treacherous ealdorman Eadric came over to their side bringing 40 English
ships with him. On the 23rd of April, 1016, Aethelred the Redeless died and
his son Edmund broke off from his harrying of Mercia to be crowned in
London. But it was a hollow ceremony and his kingdom was bounded by the
walls of London itself, for within a few days the nobles and clergy of Wessex
had sworn fealty to Knut. The summer and autumn of 1016 were occupied
by a ding-dong struggle between the two young princes, Knut the Dane and

131

A page from a register of New Minster at Winchester shows Knut the Dane, the new king of England, with his wife Aelfgifu, placing a cross on the altar there. Knut was buried at Winchester.

132

Edmund the Saxon, for the realm of England. The campaign ranged over the whole of southern England, earned Edmund the title 'Ironside' for his bravery, and ended after the fierce battle of Ashingdon in Essex, 'where perished all the flower of England'. Superficially it was 878 all over again, for the battle was followed by a treaty allotting Wessex to Edmund and the rest of England to Knut. But now the survivor would take all, and in November, 1016, very shortly after the meeting, Edmund died. As he was young and exceptionally strong and vigorous it is not impossible that he was murdered by an adherent of Knut, and tradition attributes the deed once again to the treacherous Eadric Streona.

The empire of Knut

The succession of Knut at the beginning of 1017 to the whole realm of England is the culminating point of the second Scandinavian campaign and, indeed, of 230 years of Viking enterprise. The history of England was bound to receive a new direction when the ruler of a continental country became its king; and the nature of this new direction was determined in particular by the fact that the ruler in question was also king of Denmark and Norway. For the first time in its history England became part of a political empire centred, not (as the Roman Empire had been) on the distant Mediterranean, but on its own North Sea. Without any disruptive effects the Anglian, that is to say the Scandinavian, element in her population was at last able to take its rightful place alongside the Saxon, or Germanic faction that, since the hegemony of Wessex, had tended to dominate the 'English' national character. Had this dominance persisted—had the harrying of the Danelaw initiated under Aethelred and Edmund continued under a further succession of Wessex kings—it is not impossible that the integration process of the tenth century might have taken a different direction altogether during the eleventh, and resulted in an enduring partition of England.

As it was, Knut's accession gave the country peace from external enemies and a breathing space in a new atmosphere. With his reign began the state of internal tranquillity which was from this time to be the norm rather than (as hitherto) the exception in our national history. As a king, Knut Sveinsson, Storeknut, Canute the Great (he is known to us by many names) was, during his short life, different things to different men. To the early historians of Denmark, he was a national hero, an outstanding warrior who had enlarged his inheritance and the boundaries of the Danish kingdom.

To the Norwegians he was a great and rich king who overawed people by the splendour of his court; for example, the young king proclaimed that only those who bore two-edged swords with hilts inlaid with gold would be admitted to his chosen guard! Above all, though, Knut was resented by the Norwegians for his attempt to impose Danish overlordship—not for the first or last time—on Norway. 'Does he think he will have sole rule over all northern lands? or does he think of eating up alone all the cabbages in England?' expostulates St. Olaf of Norway in *Heimskringla*.

To the southern English Knut came as a foreign conqueror only acceptable because he brought the much needed peace and good government that their own Wessex kings had latterly seemed unable to provide. To the men of the Danelaw on the other hand the recognition first of Svein then later and much more fully of Knut as kings of all England must in each case have seemed a sort of triumph for their own particular Scandinavian candidate. Despite the centuries-long integration process, many Danelaw inhabitants, perhaps especially those in Lindsey and Viking Northumbria, will still have thought of their wapentakes as an overseas extension of the old Danish homelands, and of the rest of England (especially during the recent decades) as a foreign territory in which they only lived on sufferance.

From 1017 on, however, any idea that they were England's second-class citizens will have been dispelled, first by Knut's temporary reorganization of the country, in which Northumbria and East Anglia became earldoms of an equal status with Mercia and with Wessex itself, and then in 1018 by a nationwide conference at Oxford at which 'Danes and English came to an agreement to observe Edgar's law', that is, a return to the state of good government which had last prevailed during the reign of Edgar the Peaceful (975) when both races had dwelt together on terms of perfect equality.

This conquest of England in 1016 by a ruler from overseas, was in almost all respects different from the one which was to take place just half a century later. Although obviously less acceptable to the men of Wessex than he was to his own folk in the Danelaw, Knut the Conqueror was not a 'foreigner' in the same sense that William the Conqueror would be in 1066. For one thing, unlike William, Knut spoke almost the same language as his new subjects, especially his Anglo-Danish ones. Nor did he impose on England any fresh system of government or, equally important, of land-tenure, for in this matter, despite their warlike organization the Vikings both in their homelands and the countries they settled seem (with the single exception of Normandy) to have maintained their centuries-old tradition of freedom and anti-feudalism.

Knut's character and career show to a marked degree the extraordinary assimilative, almost chameleon-like qualities evinced again and again by the Vikings. For it was as a Viking—perhaps even a pagan Viking—that the adolescent Knut had sailed up the river Trent with his father; yet within a mere five years this young man, still in his early twenties, was as much an Englishman as a Dane and would soon after be gaining a deserved reputation as a devout Christian and sincere benefactor to the English church.

So peaceful and effective was Knut's reign from 1019 that for the first time in many decades the compilers of the Anglo-Saxon Chronicle are faced with an almost total absence of stirring events to report in the English scene.

In fact most of their space, apart from that devoted to church affairs, is given to Knut's four expeditions into Scandinavia. The first of these, in 1019, was to secure his succession as king of Denmark on the death of his brother Harald. He remained there the whole winter, a fact which alone indicates the completeness of the English settlement. The second was in 1022 'to the Isle of Wight' says the Chronicle but it may well have been to some Baltic destination with a similar name. With the third campaign, conducted in 1025 or 1026, the full consequences of Knut's reconciliatory policy became apparent. Knut, like king Edgar long before him, had made a practice of taking Danes and Englishmen alike into his service in England on equal terms, the most prominent examples of Englishmen being Godwine and Leofric whom he created earls of Wessex and Mercia respectively. Now, for the first time in their history, Englishmen were prepared to fight outside their own country and side by side with Danish troops against—on this occasion— a Norwegian-Swedish force under Olaf of Norway and king Onund of Sweden: the battle place of 1026 was the mouth of Holy River (Helgaá) on the east coast of Skåne, and the outcome was indecisive.

In 1028 Knut struck a more conclusive blow against Olaf, and this year the same co-operation occurred. According to the Anglo-Saxon Chronicle, some, if not all, of the 50 ships Knut took with him belonged to 'the noblemen (thanes) of England', which was indeed a *volte-face* from earlier Viking times. The final defeat and death of Olaf occurred two years later at the battle of Stiklestad in north Norway in 1030, after which Knut reigned with unchallenged title as 'King of Englishmen, Danes, Norwegians and part of the Swedes'. Although—indeed because—he had destroyed their living king, Knut now found it politic to venerate the Norwegians' dead saint if he was to succeed as ruler of Norway.

How far should historians attribute to Knut the deliberate intention of founding a lasting Anglo-Scandinavian 'North Sea Empire'? We should be able to answer more certainly had this truly outstanding ruler not died in the prime of life. He certainly seems to have looked on his nobles and higher officials as having a currency beyond their national boundaries. His English charters were often attested by nobles from the Scandinavian provinces, and, in the other direction several English bishops (according to Adam of Bremen) were brought by Knut to serve Danish sees—among them Gerbrand to Roskilde and Reginbert to Odense. Indeed, at one point it looked as though the Danish church might become a dependent of the see of Canterbury; and though this did not happen, the powerful position it attained during the eleventh century owed a good deal to this deployment of English piety and talent across the North Sea. This movement dated back at least to the time when king Svein had employed an English bishop in Skåne and St. Olav took English priests to help him in his conversion of Norway.

In the same way not only clergy but also church practices peculiar to England were spreading to Scandinavia (including the idea that a man who built a church ought also to own it), while the erecting of churches in Denmark by masons from England accounted for a similarity of design in some of the oldest buildings of both England and Scandinavia. Only the most faithful and farseeing Christian of 789 could have predicted that the bloody and piratical onslaughts of the Vikings, aimed at the annihilation of the social order—and of the churches in particular—would end in this constructive intercourse between English and Continental churchmen and in the bringing of civilization and the Christian religion to the Norsemen's own front doors.

In the field of art, illustrated more fully in the next chapter, this new and still tenuous unity of the lands around the North Sea is symbolized by the style which was developing in all of them after the year 1000. Taking its name from the district of Ringerike in south-east Norway this art-style (in which animal ornament largely gives way to plant forms) influenced stone-carving, metalwork and manuscript decoration not just in Norway but eastwards into southern Sweden and westwards into Denmark, and, above all, into England. From the earliest times the Vikings had left their mark on English art but only in those parts of the land where they had settled. Now in the reign of Knut the influence of this latest style, the 'Ringerike', spread to the country as a whole. Its popularity and success coincided with a period when the arts in Britain were reviving after the lengthy disturbances of Aethelred's reign, and as it happened England's 'Winchester' manuscript style (itself based on Carolingian acanthus and dragon-head forms) blended very readily with Ringerike-type ornament.

Knut's court must have held many rich Anglo-Scandinavian men and women of taste and it was no doubt for one of these that the runic sarcophagus from St. Paul's (London) was carved. The sole surviving panel, the lion and serpent motif that was itself common to both Christian and Scandinavian symbolism. Further west, outside the political empire of Knut, but under similar patronage from Irish-Scandinavians, the Ringerike style was, from around 1050, the paramount influence on the decoration of ecclesiastical treasures—shrines, reliquaries and so on in Ireland.

Although Knut neither introduced new systems of land-tenure and local government nor favoured his fellow-Danes unduly at the expense of his English subjects, he will without doubt have found it necessary to reward with gifts of land, as well as of money, a considerable number of his more important Scandinavian followers. During the two decades of his rule we can therefore expect to find landowners with Viking names appearing in all parts of the country and no longer just within the confines of the Danelaw. Worcester, for example, is a county as remote from it as any, yet its bishop in 1042 finds it necessary to make the distinction between 'all the thegns in Worcestershire both English and Danish'. A Swedish investigation of the occurrence of pre-Conquest personal names in the Domesday Survey indicates that within half a century of Knut's death there were landowners

The Norwegian Ringerike style in art here ornaments the end of a sarcophagus of Knut's day found in London. ►

with Scandinavian names in every part of England — descendants in many cases of men granted estates during his reign.

Many of these grantees would have been drawn from Knut's body-guard of 3,000 huscarls and a few of their charters from him survive. Most of the evidence however comes from Domesday Book, where 33 huscarls are mentioned as holding lands 'in the time of King Edward'. These men surrounding Knut and his successors were a direct link with the wider Viking world since many of them will undoubtedly have been 'Jomsvikings' from the legendary fortress of Jomsborg in the Baltic, disbanded at the beginning of the eleventh century. Another specifically Scandinavian institution that appeared in England with Svein was the office of 'stallari' or 'staller'. Originally the man in charge of the horse-stalls and stables, this officer became under Knut and his successors second only in importance to the Chancellor. During Edward the Confessor's reign there were 8 stallers, and one of them, Eadnoth, continued under king Harald. From this Eadnoth there is a genealogical link with our own time since he was the direct male ancestor of the still-surviving English family of Berkeley.

It is significant too that the chroniclers during Knut's reign discard the old title 'ealdorman' in favour of the Norse 'jarl' (Englished as eorl or earl) for the royal officers set over a county or counties. All these considerations and others reinforce Professor Stenton's opinion that historians dealing generally with the period have probably tended to underestimate the significance of the Danish element in the Anglo-Danish state.

But 'a King is for glory not for long life' and in this respect Knut the Great was a typical Viking ruler. So much activity — much of it 'glorious' — was packed into his career that it is hard to realize that at his death on the 12th of November, 1035, he was probably still under 40 years old.

Had he lived out his allotted span of 70 years Knut might well have continued to reign over his Nordic maritime empire at least until the year 1066. Under his controlling and reconciling hand political and other circumstances in Denmark, Norway and England would certainly have been quite different; in the latter, the chain of happenings which led up to the Norman conquest need never have been linked together the way they were.

Down the intervening centuries English people (historians included) have been conditioned to attribute to the Norman conquest something of the inevitability of an act of God and to accept that the history of their country begins in 1066 with a slate miraculously wiped clean by the deeds of that fateful year. But if our study of the Viking movement in the west, and of its effects on Britain in particular, does nothing else it should enable us to see that there are other interpretations of '1066 and all that' at least as valid as the accepted one — for instance that the conquest represented the forced withdrawal of Britain from its natural (albeit still fragile) association with Denmark and the Scandinavian world and the imposition of an artificial

◄ *An independent English style in art, here on a silver cup from Denmark, had its own influence on continental design.*

139

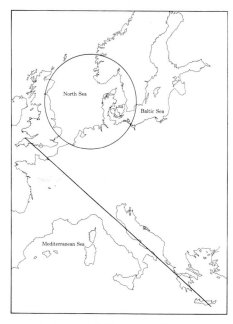

Britain lies within a circle of Scandinavian influence and on an axis with the Mediterranean world.

association with France, Germany and the countries of southern Europe. If 1066 was the beginning of an era it was just as much the end of one!

For nearly three centuries the Vikings had been the much dramatized shock-troops of a Scandinavian expansionist movement, itself the continuation of something that had begun four or five centuries earlier still. In those earlier times entire peoples (including the Angles) had been moving out of Scandinavia almost unsung by skalds and sagas and virtually unrecorded by contemporary historians. Now, towards the mid-eleventh century the whole movement, both early and late, was coming to a halt. The initiative in western Europe was passing from the Scandinavians to other nations (some of them Viking-begotten), owning different social, political and cultural allegiances from those of the Viking world. England was at the hinge, or perhaps more accurately on the tangent, of these two planes of influence and nowhere better can the shift from one to the other be seen than in this divided isle during the thirty years between Knut's death and the Norman conquest.

Like nearly all the foreigners who subsequently won the English throne, Knut had made England his main residence and had increasingly identified himself with English interests. In England he died and there, not in the Jelling dynasty's tomb at Roskilde but in the royal church of the West Saxon dynasty at Winchester, he was buried. Many great men who die too young leave inadequate successors or leave their succession in a muddle. Unfortunately Knut did both. He left three sons, and his heir to England and Denmark should have been Hordaknut, his son by Aethelred's widow Emma. However, back in 1030, Knut had installed as ruler of Norway the boy

Svein, his son by his English consort Aelfgifu. Ever since the defeat and death in that year of 'Saint' Olaf, Norwegian national feeling had been developing so strongly in favour of Olaf's son Magnus that by 1035 not only had Svein and Aelfgifu been forced to retreat from Norway to Denmark, where Svein died, but the latter country was itself being threatened by a Norwegian invasion. In these circumstances Hordaknut, who was in Denmark at Knut's death, could not risk sailing to England to claim his inheritance, and the English throne (after a period of regency from 1035–7) therefore remained in the possession of Harold, the other son of Knut and Aelfgifu.

Despite their distinguished paternity, this Harald, nicknamed 'Harefoot' was as dim and short-lived a personality as his brother Svein, and during his regency and short reign evil practices broke out once more in England as the pro-Scandinavian and pro-Wessex factions took up sides against each other.

Since 1020 the most powerful subject in England had been Godwine, jarl of Wessex. Though of Saxon parentage, Godwine's marriage to Gytha had clearly given him not only overriding Danish sympathies (their elder sons had the Viking names Svein, Harald and Tostig) but also a devotion to Knut and his policies which survived the king's death. By 1042 all Knut's sons would be dead also, but until then Godwine's chief object was to carry out his master's plans, above all by securing the continued connection between England and Denmark. Godwine supported both the Danish princes in turn: first Hordaknut, then, when he failed to arrive from Denmark, Harald Harefoot. In their interest the Saxon prince Alfred who came over in 1036 was repulsed with unnecessary severity together with his hated Norman supporters. 'Some of them were sold for money, some cruelly murdered, Some of them were put in chains, and some of them were blinded, some were mutilated and some ignominiously scalped. No more horrible deed was done in this land after the Danes came and made peace with us here' comments the Chronicle on this premature Norman invasion. And its account of Hordaknut's short reign has further echoes of the bad old days —danegelds amounting to £32,000 thinly disguised as 'a tax for the payment of the fleet' and 'all Worcestershire harried' because it had murdered two of the huscarls collecting the levy.

After Hordaknut's sudden death in 1042 the dream of Anglo-Danish unity faded away. A Norwegian king, Magnus Olafsson, now occupied the Danish throne and the only available heir to the English one seemed to be Edward, Aethelred's surviving son by Emma of Normandy. Godwine, therefore, like his fellow statesmen acclaimed Edward as king and acquiesced in the separation of England from Denmark; but this acquiescence was accompanied by a determination, shared by his sons and by many of their fellow countrymen, that England, now independent, should not fall under the domination of another neighbouring Viking power—Normandy.

'Ginna let lay this stone and also Toki' state the runes on a sarcophagus found at St Paul's in London (left). The dead man was probably a member of the court of king Knut, Ginna and Toki his widow and son. Knut fostered the traditions of England and a peaceful assimilation of some Scandinavian practices. An English manuscript of the 11th century (below) includes a typically Scandinavian intertwined beast and the sarcophagus was carved and painted in the Norwegian Ringerike style. Ringerike was found to blend well with England's Winchester style.

So for the 24 years of Edward's reign England was a vessel with two towlines aboard. On one, the king and his Norman courtiers pulled the country into the Franco–Norman orbit while on the other, grasped by Godwine and his party, the weakening forces of the Viking world sought to retain England in the circle of Scandinavia.

The threat from Normandy

The first link in the long chain of events which ended in the conquest of England was the marriage of Aethelred to Emma of Normandy in 1002. Emma herself appears to have disliked both Ethelred and her sons by him and to have much preferred her second husband Knut whom she married in 1017. From 1017 till her death in 1052 she consistently supported the Scandinavian case and its claimants to the English throne—first Hordaknut, then Magnus of Norway and after him Svein Estridsson.

Her son Edward, on the other hand, was from his earliest years pro-Norman in outlook. Not surprisingly, his long residence of forty years in Normandy made him prefer Normans to Englishmen and, although his Anglo-Danish subjects, from Godwine downwards, accepted him as king, they on their side had no real affection for Edward or for the Wessex dynasty from which he sprang.

The organization of the palace was rapidly taking on a Norman appearance and except in the matter of land tenure English government was coming more and more to resemble continental feudalism. Indeed, the Normans did not introduce as many innovations after 1066 as has generally been supposed some of the principal changes attributed to them date from Edward's reign; and during the last two decades of the Anglo-Saxon period the English court seems to have become assimilated in a number of respects to the type that prevailed in Normandy and in the neighbouring Carolingian empire.

And what of the Viking or Scandinavian sides of this parallelogram of forces? In England the doyenne of the pro-Scandinavian faction was Emma the queen mother and in 1043, her own son by Knut being dead, she may have not only invited Magnus of Norway to invade England but actually offered him her treasure in support. This would at any rate explain Edward's confiscation that year of all his mother's lands and treasures and also his depriving bishop Stigand of his see and his possessions 'because', reports the Chronicle, 'Stigand was his mother's closest confidant, and she, as was supposed, followed his advice.'

An attack by Magnus was imminent in autumn, 1047, after he had defeated Svein Estridsson, but in that year Magnus died, aged 24, from a riding accident.

Svein now became king of Denmark and Harald Hardradi king of Norway. Both regarded themselves as claimants to the English throne, but for the next 17 years both were so embroiled in a wasteful and pointless struggle with each other that there was not much risk to England of either's claim being implemented. After their mutual treaty in 1064 however, Harald Hardradi, that 'Viking to end all Vikings' lost no time in planning and launching his massive attack—it may have numbered 9,000 men with 300 ships—in September, 1066: and it nearly succeeded. Svein Estridsson delayed his Danish attempt on England (also, according to the Chronicle, with 300 ships) until the summer of 1069, and it too was initially successful. But as we all know, it was the Norman invasion from the south between these two Scandinavian campaigns which was finally and completely successful and whose outcome determined all subsequent English history.

In what respects were these Viking descendants in Normandy so different from their cousins in Norway and Denmark, and from their even closer cousins in the English Danelaw? Why should a Norman conquest, as compared with an equally conceivable Danish or Norwegian conquest, work so great and lasting a change on the corporate character of the English nation?

To these questions there are a number of related answers. The first is that, though largely Dano-Norwegian by descent, the Vikings in Normandy had become by 1066 a fundamentally different people.

Once established on Frankish territory they had increasingly identified themselves with their Frankish and Gallic neighbours, with the result that not only had their language been submerged but with it the still more precious inheritance from Scandinavian forebears of a long tradition (in a rough and ready way) of freedom and independence—freedom of speech and assembly, the liberty of the individual and the personal worth of the ordinary freeman.

Back in 905, Hrolf the Ganger's Danes may indeed have declared that they would 'never submit to the King of France or anyone else, nor accept servitude nor receive any favours except those they won for themselves in battle.' Brave sentiments! but as it turned out not able to stand up for long against the prevailing Zeitgeist to which they were exposed in Normandy, and which their leaders proved all too eager to imbibe.

Since the days of Charlemagne himself the political organization and ethos of the Carolingian territories had been operating steadily against the liberty of the ordinary individual and increasingly towards the system (or, more accurately, organized confusion) of protection rackets which we dignify with the name feudalism.

The result in Normandy was that within a century of the Viking settlement—even though feudalism had not yet fully developed—the concept of freedom and equality as the right of every common man had largely vanished beneath a centralized administration organized on a military and authoritarian basis. An example of this authoritarian attitude comes from around the year 1000, when a delegation of the duchy's inhabitants demanded their old rights of access to and use of its woodlands and waters. Its members were promptly rounded up by duke Richard's magnates and each deprived of a hand and a foot!

Domination of the peasantry by this new territorial nobility effected a notable change in the landscape of Normandy itself and eventually of those countries which the Normans conquered. The Trelleborg-style camps of Viking times were no longer the model; instead, all over the countryside, mottes—high circular mounds of earth—were raised, each topped by its wooden fortress, for which, before long, keeps and castles of stone would be substituted.

At the same time the importance of cavalry in the feudal scheme of things was altering centuries-old Viking methods of fighting. The Norman warrior *par excellence* was now no longer a foot soldier wielding battle-axe and halberd, but a mounted knight on a heavy horse, fighting with sword and spear.

This, then, was the new model of society: a mass of peasants many of them unfree, producing the agricultural surplus necessary to support a military class of squires and knights who in turn existed to serve the lesser and greater magnates, themselves the vassals of the ruler. By 1066 much of Europe (but not Scandinavia or Britain) was covered by this feudal patchwork; and by this time the Norman version had caught up with and even surpassed in thoroughness the feudalism of neighbouring states.

But their adoption of feudalism with all its implications was only one of the factors that made the Normans different from their Viking kinsmen elsewhere. Other factors were: their conversion to a Latin culture in place of a Nordic one; the adoption of French as their everyday language and of Latin as the legal and ecclesiastical one; and the very close identity of interest between church and state. For as the church in Normandy had mostly been endowed by its dukes, so they in return appointed most of the chief clerics. This not only ensured the support of the church for national policy but also meant that successive dukes of Normandy always had at their disposal the services of a number of trained clerks and administrators, making Normandy the most highly organized country in Europe at this time. Allied to this organizing efficiency were the Viking legacies—abundant energy, warlike tradition, a colonizing urge and (probably) the usual abundance of landless younger sons for whom there was little scope in Normandy itself.

The Norman conquest

This then was the people that was exploding over Europe in the eleventh century and this the power that from mid-century onwards was menacing the much larger (but less united), more civilized (but less dynamic) realm across the Channel, under a king 'whose role in English history was to prepare the way for the Norman conquest both by the little that he did and by the much that he left undone.'

Some of what the Confessor did to advance the Norman cause we have seen earlier in this chapter. One of the many things 'the holy but imbecile Edward' left undone was the consummation of his marriage with Godwine's daughter, with its consequence of a disputed succession to the English throne.

As we have seen, death had already eliminated some of the claimants, and one more—perhaps the most credible—was removed in 1057. This was Edward, son of Edmund 'Ironside', who had come over from Hungary to visit his uncle the king but had died mysteriously before reaching court. 'We do not know for what reason it was so arranged that he could not see King Edward', writes the Chronicler suspiciously. Edward left a son, Edgar the Atheling; but since he was an infant and lived in distant Hungary he seems to have been omitted from most people's calculations—though he did play some part from 1066 onward. Had the Exile and the Atheling succeeded to the throne England would at least have been linked to Europe through one of its more civilized communities, one far removed from the barbarians and philistines of Normandy.

Next comes earl Harold. On jarl Godwine's death in 1053 Harold succeeded to the earldom and to all his father's possessions, becoming in his turn the mightiest subject in England and rousing thereby the intense jealousy of Aelfgar, earl of Mercia. Harold Godwineson's genealogical claims were slight—his mother had been a connection by marriage of king Knut and his sister was the Confessor's virgin bride—but he had the advantage of being king Edward's nominated successor. Half Saxon by birth, he and his brothers appear almost wholly Viking by nature as they march and countermarch through the pages of the Chronicle harrying and plundering in England and Wales in pursuance of their father's anti-Norman policy.

Duke William, against whom this policy was chiefly directed, had a dynastic claim (even setting aside his bastardy) still weaker than Harold's, for his father had merely been Edward's cousin. William too declared that Edward had nominated him as successor—and his strongest suit in the eyes of his contemporaries was that Harold around 1064 had sworn an oath to uphold this claim and had acknowledged William as his lord.

The fourth and fifth claimants, as we have seen, were the Viking rivals Harald Hardradi and Svein Estridsson and to these should probably be added a sixth, Harald Hardradi's son Magnus Barelegs. Of the four Chronicle manuscripts covering 1058 only one mentions 'In this year came a pirate host from Norway'; only to dismiss the statement with the uninformative words 'it is tedious to tell how it all happened.' However, from Irish and Welsh sources it seems what in fact did happen in that year was a major attempt on England by Aelfgar of Mercia joined to a resurgence of the Celtic–Norse 'auld alliance' led by Gruffydd ap Llewelyn the Welsh king and Magnus Barelegs Haraldsson.

The latest event of Edward's troubled reign was a revolt by Viking Northumbria in autumn, 1065, when the northern Danelaw threw out Harold's brother Tostig and took as their jarl Aelfgar of Mercia's son Morcar; this revolt was accompanied by a large-scale Northumbrian invasion of the midlands, the northcountrymen, in old Viking style, carrying off all the livestock they could find, amounting to many thousands, taking many hundreds of captives and carrying them off north with them. Looked at with hindsight it can be seen as the earliest of the many revolts in which Scandinavian northerners, in the years and centuries succeeding the conquest, would protest—usually in vain—against domination of England by Saxon southerners, and express their often well-founded suspicions of the new-fangled modes of thought, religion, speech and government that the south would continue to impose on them!

Edward Confessor died on the 5th of January, 1066. The events of the fateful twelvemonth following have been rehearsed in a thousand textbooks and a million classrooms over the English-speaking world. In the present narrative we shall therefore only look at them in relation to the Viking story.

On the day of Edward's burial (the 6th of January) Harold God-wineson was consecrated king of England. The loss of Northumbria by his brother Tostig naturally weakened Harold's footing in the north, and while in exile Tostig further damaged his brother's position by associating himself with England's enemies, duke William (whose duchess was Tostig's niece) and Harald Hardradi.

In May, 1066 (heralded by Halley's comet), the Norwegian invasion of England began with raids and harrying by a fleet of Orkney (and therefore Norway-controlled) Vikings on the south and east coasts, in which Tostig was involved. Late in August this force, with only 12 ships, retreated to Scotland where Tostig (says the Chronicle) 'was met by Harald the Norwegian king with 300 ships, to whom Tostig gave allegiance. Together they sailed into the Humber [and up the Ouse] until they came to York, where earl Morcar [of Northumbria] and earl Edwin [of Mercia] fought against them, and the Norwegian king gained the victory.' This was the Battle of Gate Fulford fought on the 20th of September a mile and a half south of York. As might be expected this city welcomed the Norwegians. 'After the battle' (continues the Chronicle) 'Harald of Norway and earl Tostig entered York and received hostages from the borough, besides assistance in the way of provisions, and so retired thence to their ships [moored in the Ouse at Riccall 10 miles south of York]. They offered to conclude an abiding peace with the citizens provided they all marched southwards with them to conquer this realm.'

Not only the citizens of York but the thegns of the whole of Yorkshire seem to have willingly agreed to co-operate with this project and to provide hostages. To await these at a more convenient gathering place the Norwegian army moved away from the Ouse marshlands to a point 7 miles east of York and about 13 miles across country from their ships. They camped on the east bank of the river Derwent where it was crossed by the Roman road from York to the coast; by 1066 the original stone-paved ford (Stamford) had been replaced by a wooden bridge. Harald Hardradi seemed to have no inkling of the English army's approach—in the Eddaic poem attributed to him he is made to exclaim: 'Helmets do shine, but I have not mine. All our byrnies [mail-coats] are down at the ships.'

The Battle of Stamford Bridge (Monday the 25th of September, 1066) has never been told more succinctly than by the Chronicle: 'Meanwhile came Harald the king of the English with all his levies on the Sunday to Tadcaster . . . and on the Monday he marched through York and came upon them unawares beyond the bridge. They joined battle and fierce fighting went on until late in the day; and there Harald king of Norway was slain and earl Tostig and countless numbers of men with them, both English and Norwegians' [which seems to imply that numerous Yorkshiremen besides the hostages had already joined the Norwegians]. 'The remaining Norwegians were put to flight while the English fiercely assailed their rear, until some of them reached their ships. Some were drowned, others burnt to death and thus perished in various ways so that there were few survivors. . . . The king then gave quarter to Olaf (Kyrre) the son of the King of the Norwegians, to their bishop, to the Jarl of Orkney and to all those who were left aboard their ships. They then went inland to our king, and swore oaths that they would ever maintain peace and friendship with this land; and the king let them sail home with 24 ships.' One indication of the huge Norwegian loss of life is that, of an army which had arrived in a total of 312 ships, this remnant were able to pack themselves into a mere 24. This was the Norsemen's second pitched battle within five days and it ended for ever any serious challenge on the part of the Norwegian Vikings to wield authority in England. But we must remember that, until they actually arrived on the battlefield of Hastings, duke William cannot have known whether he would be facing an English army or a Norwegian one; and that, in defeating Harald Hardradi, the English king had not only relieved the duke of Normandy of his most formidable rival, but, by the heavy loss of huscarls at Stamford Bridge, also reduced his own chances of standing up to the Norman invaders—who at that very moment were crossing the Channel. As for the forces of Edwin and Morcar, they had been so decimated at Fulford that they never even arrived to take part in the Battle of Hastings.

As a tailpiece to the battle, *Heimskringla* has an anecdote that throws a timeless gleam of light on to that late September Monday evening in 1066. One of the Norwegians is making his way across country to the ships; like many of his comrades he has been fighting in his shirt sleeves and is chilled by the autumn evening. He meets an East Riding farmer, wearing a thick

Harold unwisely swears to support William of Normandy's claim to the English throne.

Edward the Confessor dies. The English crown is Harold's.

A bad omen. A comet. And king Harold sees the ghosts of an invasion fleet.

The Norman army crosses to Hastings.

sheepskin jacket, and asks if he will sell it to him. 'No, for I can tell by your speech that you are a Norwegian and I ought to kill you if I can, not clothe you.' Whereupon the Viking cuts off the farmer's head and appropriates his coat. Whatever the moral of the story it seems to indicate that, though not all the inhabitants of Yorkshire favoured Harald Hardradi, a Danelaw farmer and a Norwegian Viking were at least still able, in the late eleventh century, to converse with each other without difficulty. This would certainly not have been the case in, for example, Sussex.

Vikings under Norman rule

Like Caesar's Gaul, England in 1066 was divided into three parts. These divisions were founded on the different legal customs observed in the Danelaw, Mercia and Wessex respectively. However, since the differences between the latter two were inconsiderable, the real division was between the Danelaw and the rest of England. Since our last look at it the Danelaw would seem to have extended its territory south-westward but this does not necessarily mean any large-scale colonization of, for example, Hertfordshire and Buckinghamshire by men of Viking stock, merely that Danish custom and law had spread to those areas and with them Scandinavian ways of thought and speech, including the important and new idea that a majority vote must prevail where an assembly has a difference of opinion.

What was it about the nature of the Danelaw that was already, on the eve of the Norman conquest, so firmly established as to enable it to be a leaven in the English lump and a reservoir of the Anglo-Scandinavian spirit in many of the flat and arid times which would follow that not altogether propitious event? In general terms perhaps the best answer is given by Messrs. Foote and Wilson: 'Freedom of speech and personal liberty were inherited by the greater part of the population of the Scandinavian countries. We may say that in the earlier part of our period this freedom was more of a fact and less of an ideal than was the case in the thirteenth century and later . . . even so, feudalizing forces never totally destroyed a sturdy range of recalcitrant and conservative farmers, whose views on the rights of man, especially when linked with the rights of the property-owner and rate-payer, build some sort of a bridge between the "democracy" of the Viking age and the "democracy" of our own.'

No analysis of England's own 'Scandinavian country' could ever be undertaken without reference to the Danelaw's chief and most able apologists, Professors F. M. and D. M. Stenton, in such works as *The Danes in England* and *The Free Peasantry of the Northern Danelaw*. Their main contention is that sources—particularly Domesday Book—of the eleventh and twelfth centuries reveal in Scandinavian England the survival of a free peasant population to which there is no true parallel in the south and west of the country. In most of England the Norman clerks compiling the

Domesday information recognize only villeins, bordars and cottagers, all with holdings of land on a very small scale. In the Danelaw they were of necessity forced to recognize a higher class of freeholder, for whom they used the word 'sokeman', still perhaps holding only 30 acres or so but much more independent of manorial disciplines and having the responsibility for paying their own taxes. 'The most distinctive feature of the early medieval economy of the Danelaw is the great body of peasants who individually enjoyed personal independence.'

A closer analysis reveals that this class was most numerous in East Anglia, Yorkshire and the area between these two referred to before the conquest as the territory of the Five (sometimes Seven) Boroughs. Mainly as a result of two centuries of spadework by Danish settlers, these were the wealthiest and most populous counties in England.

William the Norman succeeded in imposing his rule on Wessex during 1067, and in 1068 'when the king was informed that the people in the north had gathered together and would oppose him if he came, he marched to Nottingham and built a castle there and so on to York and built two castles there.'

During 1068 the Northumbrians had already slain William's Saxon nominee to its earldom, so later that year he dispatched one of his Normans, Robert de Comines, to the post, with a strong force of mercenaries in support. Arriving at Durham in mid-winter they unwisely occupied the tiny peninsular borough and were there cut off, and 900 soldiers were massacred by the Anglian inhabitants. This was the signal for all Northumbria, both Anglian and Scandinavian, to rise. York was the natural rallying place and the boy prince Edgar Atheling was fetched down from Scotland as their figurehead. 'But William came unexpectedly upon them from the south with an overwhelming host and routed them and slew several hundreds of those who could not escape. . . . The prince returned again to Scotland.'

The last Viking raids

Though their outcome was ineffective, these events indicate how strong a flame of resistance burned in the northern Danelaw against the conquest of England by Norman William and his 'bandits league'. It only needed this internal opposition to be reinforced by some formidable external power for a real test to be made of the strength of the Norman hold on England. This came in the autumn of 1069 when king Svein Estridsson of Denmark made his bid (as the successor of his uncle, Knut the Great) to the English throne. Having seen the inadequacy of Edgar Atheling many English leaders, especially in the North, will have pinned their hopes on Svein as the Danish Viking heir and may indeed have offered him the English crown. If so, Svein did not immediately come to win it in person. The Chronicle tells us: 'Ealdred, Archbishop of York died on Sept. 11th 1069. Soon thereafter three sons of King Svein with 240 ships came from Denmark into the Humber, and with them Jarl Osbern (Svein's brother, previously resident in England) and Jarl Thorkill. There they were met by Prince Edgar, Earl Waltheof, Maerlesvein and Jarl Thorkill (all northern magnates) with the Northumbrians and all the people of the country. Forming an immense host, riding and marching in high spirits they all resolutely advanced on York and stormed and destroyed the castle. . . .'

Alas, it was many a long decade before 'high spirits' were again to be the norm in the Ridings of Yorkshire! For, finding the Danes and Northumbrians firmly entrenched in York, William carried out (but in a still more savage manner) the same strategy that had won him London in 1066, namely the total devastation and destruction of the countryside around the city. Unable to find food the Danish troops withdrew from York to their ships in the Humber and before Christmas William and his mercenaries had re-occupied the capital of Northumbria.

The king was plainly aware how near to failure the northern revolt, aided by Denmark, could have brought his original plans for government of England as an Anglo-Norman state; government that is, with at least a semblance of consultation and consent from the conquered English. But whatever his use hitherto of the velvet glove it was in fact on force and military organization that William's authority finally rested and now the iron hand was to be exerted with a vengeance and ferocity which were the measure of his exasperation, sense of failure and the scare that the Northumbrians had given him.

This explains why what had begun as a tactical strategy did not end when its object—the capitulation of York—was achieved, but was continued throughout the winter of 1069 and spring of 1070 as a deliberate policy of 'frightfulness'. The objective was nothing less than the destruction of life and the means of life in northern England from Trent to Tees and extending into parts of Mercia. 'It was,' says Professor Stenton, 'a deliberate attempt to ruin the population of the affected districts . . . and to secure that neither Mercia nor Northumbria should ever revolt again.' Indeed from this moment those ancient jarldoms, formerly kingdoms, vanished for ever.

It was long—perhaps a century or more—before Yorkshire recovered from the Conqueror's savage devastation. In some parts scarcely a homestead had escaped burning, scarcely a human being was left alive that William's horsemen could search out. And in that grim winter of 1069–70 many thousands that survived the sword will have died from exposure and famine. Sixteen years later the Domesday Book entries from this area testify to the scale of the destruction—many scores of villages with their names and descriptions followed by the stark message: *et vasta est*—'and it is waste'. Scores more, valued 'in the time of King Edward' at £30 or £40, were now reckoned at a few shillings, or at nothing; many places had no inhabitants left at all.

A high proportion of those killed or driven out will have been descendants of the Danish Viking settlers but, since their places may have been filled by Norwegians from Cumbria and Lancashire moving across to the east, the total area of Scandinavian settlement was not perhaps greatly diminished. Those that survived, or re-settled, had from now on to accept a feudalized state of society and a Normanized ruling class—for William seized this opportunity to replace the jarls and thegns of the old Danelaw with Norman adventurers for whom up to now he had not been able to find sufficient forfeited land to reward them the way they desired.

And what of the Danish invasion fleet whose 'Viking greed for prisoners and money' had allowed William to re-take York? After sitting all the winter in the Humber-Isle of Axholme area they were joined in spring, 1070 by king Svein and thereafter by an increasing number of Englishmen from the southern Danelaw, prominent among them Hereward the Wake. One version of the Chronicle describes in minute detail (understandably, since it was written there) a successful raid on Peterborough and the occupation of Ely, after which William and Svein came to terms and the Danish troops eventually sailed for home.

In autumn, 1074, after Svein Estridsson's long reign had ended, his younger son 'Saint' Knut, with 200 ships, staged an abortive invasion of England in support of a rebellion against William; and, raids apart, this was the last Scandinavian attempt for centuries to come to sway the destinies of the island they had so nearly succeeded in annexing to their own Nordic world. For over a thousand years, however, marriage connections between the ruling families of England and Scandinavia, especially Denmark, have contributed to the harmony and understanding that has generally existed between these nations since the time of Knut the Great. To those who cherish the relationship it is a matter for mutual satisfaction that a direct descendant (on his father's side) of the Royal House of Denmark is now heir to the throne of Scotland and England.

Chapter VII **Viking Life**

To blow away some of the mist and mystique in which the Viking inhabitants of Scandinavia have so often been enveloped, we have shown them in their geographical and historical setting and in the light of common day, dispelling the quasi-supernatural character they have acquired and revealing them as human beings (even though exceptional ones) in a verifiable human context and struggling with humanity's perennial problems. This chapter will fill in some details of their social and cultural background.

Slavery

Snorri Sturluson's *Heimskringla*, already referred to in these chapters, draws a convincing picture of the social economy in his account of a Norwegian 'landed man' called Erling Skjalgson in the early eleventh century: 'Erling had always 30 thralls at home in his houses, besides other servants. He set his thralls to daywork and gave them time afterwards and allowed every man to work for himself at dusk or in the night. He gave them acres to sow corn thereon for themselves; . . . he set a price and ransom on every one of them, and many freed themselves the first year or the second—all who were thrifty enough had freed themselves in three years. With this money Erling bought himself other thralls. Some of his freed men he turned to herring fishing and some to other trades. Some cleared woods and built themselves farms there, and to all of them he gave a good start in one way or another.'

Since, in this passage, Snorri is not involved in comparative chronology or grinding any of his political axes his description is probably a reliable one. If so, it confirms the ubiquitousness of a money economy in Scandinavia at this time, and (unless Erling was exceptional in his treatment of thralls) indicates that slavery was not the hopeless or irremediable condition it is

On a good sword the Vikings lavished much of their taste for ▶
richness—this one has been elegantly finished in silver.

often assumed to be, at least where the slave was 'homebred'—a member of the same race and society as his owner and not merely an item of merchandise. For one cannot imagine the Viking trader in Russia giving his Wendish or Slav captives a similar opportunity to free themselves! But, at the other extreme, homebred thralls in Sweden could have a dwelling and livestock of their own and both there and among the relatively democratic colonists of Iceland they had certain rights if injured or if their wives or daughters were seduced. Slaves—many of them Irish—are frequently referred to in the Icelandic sagas, but, after the farming land was taken up, their numbers decreased because landless freemen were now looking for jobs.

We should not underestimate the numbers of slaves in the Viking world. For a landowner like Erling Skjalgson to keep up a stock of 30 was apparently normal and there must have been others like him with this many slaves or more. Smaller landowners were of course still more numerous and they too might each own up to an average of half a dozen slaves. (On the face of it the Frostathing law's allocation of 3 slaves to even a 12-cow farm looks excessive, but northern Norway would have a low stock/acreage ratio and 12 cows with followers could represent a herd of 25–30, not to mention other livestock.) Slavery continued on a diminishing scale in Iceland at least until the end of the Viking period, but in the rest of Scandinavia survived for up to a further two centuries.

The fact that a country is 'Christian' has unfortunately never been a guarantee of its outlawing slavery, especially where there are strong economic motives in its favour—witness England from the eighth to the fourteenth century and from the sixteenth to the nineteenth. But, having said this, one must also recognize that often the chief factor in the decline of slavery has been the coming of Christianity.

In theory, at least, the church does not discriminate between the free and the unfree. Its rites of baptism and marriage are therefore as binding on slaves as on others, and a Christian slave-owner would have to recognize their sanctity. He could, for example, no longer control his slaves' birth rate by exposing their new-born children or by castration, and besides putting a stop to these and other specific malpractices Christianity gradually introduced a new spirit of humanity which must in time have steadily improved the conditions of the slave and sweetened his relationships both with his master and with his fellow men and women. For example, in Christian Iceland an owner was obliged to provide for a slave who had become incapable, whereas previously he could—at least in theory—be put down like a sick animal.

One of the merits of Viking society was that, once a man became free, his feet were placed securely on a ladder up which his energy and skill could take him and his family to any level in the community. First, however, over most of Scandinavia, custom demanded that the ex-slave should make his

◄ *Runic memorial stones sometimes include details of the dead man's life—services to the community or exploits overseas.*

entry into society by becoming either a member of a family or at least a legal member of the community; for it was his non-membership of these that had made his previous existence legally null and void.

Freed men

In the more traditional parts of Scandinavia, such as western and northern Norway under the Gulathing and Frostathing laws, graduation from slavery to freedom involved a probationary period which might extend in theory—but surely seldom in practice?—over four generations. During this period the ex-slave and his family would remain clients of their former master, owing him respect and the performance of certain duties. Elsewhere the process might be speeded up by his providing a 'freedom-feast' in his master's honour.

That a freedman could feel lasting gratitude is proved by the runic inscription of about 1050 from the stave church at Hørning (near Randers) in Denmark: 'Toki the smith raised this stone in memory of Thorgisl Gudmundarson, who gave him gold and liberty'. Men who had attained full freedom were called *leysingi* and were a class significant enough to give rise to a number of Danelaw place-names; while in Norway Christian law assigned them an honourable place (near the church) when they were buried.

The free

Over the whole Viking world free men had certain basic rights, common to all: the right to full benefit from the law, to attend the 'thing', to take part in public affairs, and to bear arms. After this, varying economic circumstances or the performing of an official function gave men a different standing one from another, and therefore different rights. The situation varied from country to country and century to century. But two terms for free men were in general use.

First came the *bondi* who over all the areas of Scandinavian settlement signified a man owning his own house and land: a freeholder however small. Join him to his house (*hus*) and he becomes a husbond or husband, the master (so tradition has it) and male head of the household. (In England, though the expanded word 'husbandman' long retained its proper meaning of 'small farmer', *bond* was also early confused with 'bonds' so that a bondman came to mean just the opposite—a villein or serf.) Although jarls and holders of high office might have had a different status, the whole class of free men from the smallholder to the great estate owner was theoretically undivided—all were *bondi*.

The second term in general use (though introduced late into Iceland) was *hauldr*, in English 'hold'. This was used for all the larger owners of free, inalienable ancestral land. The *hauldr* had a higher atonement or compensation value than the *bondi* and in Norway enjoyed various privileges beyond those of other free men. In Viking England the class of holds included all the higher yeomanry with ancestral estates, among them men of great territorial power. Although it is hard to believe that any single hold could have given his name to the great Yorkshire seigniory of Holderness, nevertheless the hold could clearly be an officer of high rank in the Danelaw with a wergild or compensation twice as great as that of a thegn or a priest.

Among the free, there were the usual number of terms describing tenants of farms, farm managers, farm workmen, craftsmen, as well as members of the various learned professions. Another large terminology existed for the armed forces, and two of particular interest here are *thegn* and *dreng*—the former identifiable with English 'thane', while the latter survives (spelt 'Dring') as a not uncommon north of England surname. Both these terms for freemen were somewhat ill-defined and both are used in civilian as well as service contexts. The thegn is always the senior of the two: he is the head of the family, 'the squire' or, in military terms, the veteran, while the dreng is a youth, a lad, 'one of the boys', usually in the context of service in the here or in a ship's crew; for drengs were of the age-group which very much prefers team activities to sweating out the summer on an isolated farm, and of these activities the best of all was to down tools and go a-viking.

There is some argument about the status of the thegn—was he a royal official with land, as he often was in England, or did he mostly hold his estates independent of the king and everybody else? 'Dreng' at its best carries an almost ethical value—'a perfect gentleman' or 'everything a young man ought to be'; but we cannot doubt that this age-group also contained delinquents and even criminals, who left their country for their country's good and whose excesses of violence and brutality earned the Vikings the bad name they have never lost.

In England before the Norman conquest the very numerous class of thegns were the equivalent of what would later be called 'the gentry' as distinguished from the rest of the population. This did not mean they were rich—some of them had only very small estates, and needed to put themselves under the protection of more powerful landowners, though as yet without any of the obligations which the feudal system would later impose. Indeed, the traditions and natural instincts of the Viking world were wholly against feudalism and all that it stood for. With all its many faults Viking society championed the interests of the individual freeman, and had very little in common with the royal and aristocratic feudal principle that was insidiously creeping over Europe.

Women and family life
Much of this study of the Vikings has been about men and has been couched in masculine terms—the very nature of the subject matter tends in this

direction. Whatever the position of her husband, a Viking woman had no explicit political rights and not very many legal ones either—though if necessary she could speak her divorce; she could also be outlawed or executed! Her rights in the family and in the inheritance of property were entirely subordinated to those of her brothers, though from the eleventh century onwards unmarried Danish girls might get a half-sized share, and a married one could of course normally be reckoned to have received her portion as dowry. Unmarried or married she was always under tutelage, first of her father (or a guardian), then of her husband. In some laws a wife and her lover could be killed out of hand if taken in adultery, but her husband could keep any number of concubines without penalty. 'The mother I have given to my sons has transmitted to them a valiant heart' cries one Viking leader and it illustrates their curiously inverted view of the female role. Though not required to be a heroine herself the Viking girl must be the potential mother of heroes! Only as a widow did a woman attain some degree of independence and possession of her own property, including some say in whether or not she would marry again. It was, indeed, essentially a masculine society and whereas, as we have seen, its other second-class citizens, the thralls, benefited noticeably by the coming of Christianity, Scandinavian women may even have lost some of the freedom (e.g. divorce) they had in pagan times, though they did now have a chance of avoiding a thoroughly objectionable marriage by 'taking the veil'.

Although this was the ostensible state of women in Viking society, for most of them the reality may have been very different, depending as it always does on individual human circumstances and other imponderables. We know what importance Viking society attached to the family as an institution and this in itself may have inclined its members towards a correspondingly strong liking for the domestic aspects of family life, whenever they were at home to enjoy them. 'Far from home is far from joy' says an exiled Icelander. Inside the home the housewife was in charge of staff and of household possessions; and beyond this, in countless cases, mutual love and affection between husband and wife will have been what really governed relationships and determined each partner's status, irrespective of anything 'society' might lay down. However much the men might be absent, Viking self-sufficiency was based on women working at home all the year round. For children the existence of the extended family and the habit of family visiting must have helped to offset the frequent absences from home of their fathers, and, as in any community where the husband is frequently absent for long periods, the authority of the wife must have been effective in ordering and administering the family, especially where the household was an isolated one. Even in pre-Christian society, with its strongly polygamous tendency, there seems to have been, judging from the sagas, at least a scattering of emancipated Viking women capable of exerting a power (not invariably for good!) in the land.

Precious metals, acquired by the Vikings from far and wide, both lawfully and otherwise, were skilfully worked into adornment for their womenfolk—here a gold brooch and a silver ring, both from Denmark. The men were keen on their appearance too, if an English chronicler's account of their bathing habits is to be believed. The many Viking combs that have been found tally with his report that they did their hair every day.

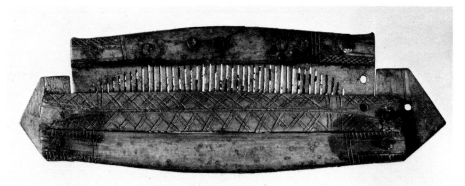

Sex

By denying feminine values in general and feminine characteristics in the male in particular, the Vikings forced the sexes into two opposing camps, reducing the potential contribution to their community of males and females alike.

These in the long view, are the grounds of our chief indictment of Viking society (and one that a good many other societies, including the Arab, would share). Some of them may result from their ambivalent attitude to sex, which on the one hand (as we saw with the Rus) was extremely explicit and forthright and on the other verged on the modest and puritanical. As an example of the latter, girls were kept in strict segregation; in Iceland even praising them in verse was punishable with outlawry; though Egil's Saga tells of a man, whose girl will not have him, cutting secret runes on a piece of whalebone and putting it in her bed to seduce her by magic. Then there is a list of 'touching fines' from the Gotland law of Sweden:

	Fine (in ozs. of silver)
Touching a woman's wrist or ankle	4 ozs.
Touching elbow, or leg between knee and calf	$2\frac{2}{3}$ ozs.
Taking hold of shoulder or just above knee	$1\frac{2}{3}$ ozs.
Touching breast	1 oz.
Touching higher still above knee (Touch dishonourable or fool's clasp. Most women put up with it when it goes that far.)	No money payable

At the other extreme one gets the impression that the sexuality of the typical Viking warrior often extended (as Nietzsche puts it) 'into the highest pinnacle of his spirit', giving rise to sentiments like the one expressed in the poem (c. 1150) *Krákumál*: 'He who has deserved the favours of a virgin throws himself intrepidly into the mélée.' Frey is the god of warriors just as much as Odin or Thor; the poem *Skírnismál* is 'instinct with sexual passion and masculine wish-fulfilment and conveys a compelling idea of the powers associated with Frey'. Another poem, *Hrafnsmál*, celebrates the glorious life of Harald Fairhair's warriors 'endowed with money and fine swords . . . and with girls from the east'. The social and sexual habits of Viking Scandinavia probably tended towards a steady increase of population, at least until the tenth century. A later writer explains the Viking expansion: 'Each of these peoples who front the North are like a mighty hive, which by the vigour of propagation and health of climate grew too full of people.' And Johannes Brøndsted considered that, with their teams of concubines, mistresses and under-wives, 'The Vikings rather prided themselves on the number of sons they could beget.' Sons were proof of a man's virility: when Njal the Icelander was taunted as 'Old Beardless—for few can tell by looking at him whether he is a man or woman' his son responds, 'It is wrong to mock him in his old age, and no real man has ever done that before. You can be quite sure that he is a man for he has fathered sons on his wife.'

As in all ages, sex was made use of by men and women for bargaining purposes: 'If you let him down you had better realise you will never be allowed in my bed again', says one wife to her husband, while the warrior Hrut, another character in Njal's Saga, readily obeys queen Gunnhild ('You shall lie with me in the upper chamber tonight with no one else present') in order to enlist her aid in collecting his Norwegian inheritance. The same Gunnhild is credited with placing her lover under a very unusual sexual spell, and these and sexual taunts abound in Viking literature. The whole sequence of events in Kormak's Saga springs from his bewitchment 'so that he and Steingerd should never have one another'.

Not only Arab observers commented on Scandinavian sexual habits. The historian Adam of Bremen had considerable respect for Svein Estridsson, his informant on so many matters, and was inclined to overlook his notorious sexual indulgences as being a weakness for which he was personally not responsible, since it was an innate susceptibility of the whole Danish nation, and of the Swedes as well. John of Wallingford tells us in his Chronicle that one reason the Danes were disliked in Wessex was their habit of combing their hair every day and taking a bath every Saturday—'by many such frivolous devices, they set off their persons, and in this manner laid siege to the virtue of the women'.

Although the Swedes were his particular adherents, Frey was worshipped, as was his voluptuous sister Freyja, all over pagan Scandinavia. The fact that Frey and Freyja symbolized fertility and the natural increase of the race would appear to be strong evidence that the Vikings were normally heterosexual—and this certainly seems to be confirmed by the various contemporary observers of their sexual activities. Evidence as to homosexual practices seems to be lacking, but given the military organization of the Vikings and their way of life when on campaign they are hardly likely to have been unknown. One inversion, that of a man playing the female role in the sexual act, is referred to in at least three of the sagas and formed part of a wizard's training (undergone by no less a personage than Odin himself). Since it is specifically black-listed as yet another of the practices banned by Christianity the number of sorcerers' apprentices at any given time must have been considerable.

Religion and superstition
Odin (whose name corresponds to the Old English Woden) was the undisputed principal deity in Norse mythology, and, as All-Father, is the link between polytheism and the one God of Christianity, particularly since of all the Norse pantheon it is Odin who is associated with spiritual and

psychic power and with omniscience. The other gods live on terms of some equality with the world of men and regularly give their names to human settlements. Not so Odin; he is the hanged God, spending nine days and nights on the gallows in his pursuit of wisdom.

This wisdom, the knowledge of runes and the mysteries of poetry he passes on to those human beings able to learn them—some of it is gathered in the stanzas known as 'Havamal'. But Odin is capricious, unpredictable, not to be relied on, so men attributed to him not only the good gifts of life but also its tragic events and undeserved afflictions. In Egil's Saga the poet Snorri Sturluson puts in the mouth of Egil Skallagrinsson, whose son Bǫdvar was drowned, two dozen stanzas 'On the loss of sons' which express the ambivalence both of Odin and of those who worship him. Egil first reproaches the god: 'I stood well with Odin, I set my trust on him, until I saw him destroy our friendship'—and then in the next verses thanks Odin for giving him 'in a good hour, the unblemished faculty of poetry'.

The Icelander, Njal, already referred to, was just the type of religious mystic to adhere to the Odin cult, and, when the time came, to make the easy transition from Odin to Christ. 'In my opinion the new faith is much better; happy the man who receives it. And if the men who spread this faith come to Iceland, I shall do all I can to further it.' He said this on many occasions (we are speaking of the 990s) 'and often would leave the company of others and meditate aloud'.

For ordinary mortals who were neither poets nor mystics, a much more popular and compatible deity was Thor. As a god, he was second only to Odin, but along with his mighty powers he had certain down-to-earth qualities which endeared him to the common man. Protector of the earth, he was also ruler of the sky, and from his name come all the Scandinavian and Germanic words for 'thunder'; his symbolic hammer *Mjollnir* was the lightning. Thor was less a transcendental godhead, more an earth-dwelling red-bearded fighting man—a super-warrior with whom the ordinary Viking soldier or *bondi* could identify himself. It is significant that the element in Old Norse religion which provided the main resistance to Christianity was the physical force of Thor, not the spiritual power of Odin, so that when the Iceland missionary Thangbrand's ship *Bison* was wrecked, it was Thor and his minions to whom the pagans gave the credit.

It was Thor's giant-killing hammer
That smashed the ocean-striding *Bison*
It was our gods who drove
The bell-ringers boat ashore
Your Christ could not save
This buffalo of the sea from destruction
I do not think your God
Kept guard over him at all!

Perhaps not so many converts retained a respectful fear of their ancient gods as we might expect, and one recent convert came down on the other side: 'I don't mind mocking the Gods, for I think that Freyja is a bitch. It must be one of the other—Odin is a dog or else Frey'.

Alongside Frey, Odin and Thor, there co-existed a number of lesser but still important deities, whose doings are celebrated in the *Völuspá* or 'Sybil's Prophecy'. These included Ull, Ty, Njord and Odin's good and beautiful son Baldur, who was killed by his blind brother Hod. Then there is the White God, Heimdall, the immaculate deity, born before all worlds, who, as watchman of the Gods, sees and hears all things, 'lying awake at night listening to the grass growing all over the world'. As Baldur and Heimdall are the incarnation of good, so Loki, the father of mischief and lies, represents the powers of evil in the world, Loki who both abets and hinders the other Gods and is kept chained until *Ragnarök* the universal destruction, when he is slain by Heimdall.

In the Viking cosmology the gods inhabited Asgard, but the home of human kind was Midgard, situated in the midst of the world, and protected by a circular wall from the land of the Jötuns, that wild and lawless country that lay around the shores of the infinite ocean. Above Midgard spread the roots of the ash tree, Yggdrasil, the centre of the Universe, under whose branches the high Gods sat daily in judgement. The boughs of Yggdrasil covered the heavens and its roots roofed over the three divisions of the lower world; it was the embodiment of vital nature, its branches swayed by the divine forces which dwelt in it. On top of Yggdrasil was an eagle, emblem of spiritual power, at its roots, constantly gnawing them away, Nidhögg, the dragon of death. Up and down its trunk ran the squirrel, Ratatösk, between the eagle and the dragon, life and death, light and darkness. The constant struggle of good and evil and the forces of destiny in which all mankind is involved were further symbolized by the two groups of Norns, the Good and the Evil, who minister to the Gods under Yggdrasil's branches. 'Nothing' Ragnar Lodbrok is made to exclaim in *Krákumál*, 'nothing can gainsay the decrees of the Norns, it is clear to me that we are all the slaves of destiny'.

Christianity
The Viking religion was a generally faithful expression of the mentality of a warlike caste, portraying itself with all its violence, passion and lusts. But, insofar as the popular religion of a people mirrors (albeit with some distortion) its own beliefs and moral conscience and its deities are larger-than-life embodiments of its own human attributes, it seems clear that the collective Viking mind was in several aspects ready for the teaching of Christianity. The belief, for example, that after the universal destruction evil (Loki) would be vanquished and only the good deities would be reborn (with the hint too of a single Almighty Being ruling henceforth in

At Uppsala (top) three pagan royal burial mounds were still a centre for heathen worship a century after Sweden's conversion to Christianity. Thor's hammers and valkyries were familiar pagan talismans (left and above) but one mould-maker began to provide for Christian crosses too (left). Church bells (below left) were thought to frighten off the heathen spirits— shown here as the gods Odin, Thor and Frey (below right).

peace) was something on which the Christian missionaries could readily base their teaching; and the fact that in a polytheistic religion there is no difficulty about adding one more God to those already on the list must have been a help to them, at least in the initial stages.

It was to accommodate this open frame of mind that missionaries permitted and perhaps encouraged *primsigning* which involved neither full instruction nor baptism but simply making the sign of the cross over the candidate and no doubt the handing out of a crucifix to add to his existing collection of amulets. By this method a pagan Viking could take Christianity 'on appro.' without committing himself or renouncing (and angering) his existing gods; being able to associate and trade with both Christian and heathen on equal terms no doubt appealed to his penchant for making the best of both worlds. Superficially at least there is not a great deal of difference between Thor's hammer and Christ's cross and there is one mould in the Copenhagen museum designed for the production (in a ratio of two to one) both of crosses and hammers.

The Saga of the Faroe Islanders has an account of not just the *primsigning* but the conversion of a young Viking, Sigmund Brestesson, around the year 997. The missionary in this instance was no less a person that the king of Norway himself, the famed Olaf Tryggvason. 'And now above all', says the king to Sigmund, 'inasmuch as I have heard that thou hast never slain offerings to false gods after other mens' guise I therefore have hope that the High King of Heaven, maker of all things will lead thee by my words to the knowledge of his Holy Name and Holy Faith, and make thee my fellow in the right faith as thou art my match in strength and in all feats of skill.'

King Olaf's sentiments perhaps owe something to the rather later date of the saga's actual composition, but Sigmund's reply has an authentic ring and may well voice what thousands of Viking converts must have thought or felt: 'As far as I can guess from your fair words this faith you hold is in all ways better and more beauteous than that which heathen men hold—and I would not offer sacrifices to false gods because I saw long ago that usage was no good, though I knew none better.' To the practical Viking mind the efficacy of the new religion was an important consideration, and one thing that would specially appeal to their strong sense of history was the fact that the life of Christ and the redemption of the world could be located in a firm spatio-temporal framework—something utterly impossible in the case of their own dateless mythologies! Moreover, the very tenets which are unpalatable to Christians today—the dogmas, the limited time-scale, the dubious genealogies—were just those to appeal to people 'hot for certain-ties' like the Vikings, as also were the firm answers given by the missionaries on the purpose of life, on death, and on the after-life.

Although Sigmund Brestesson says he made no use of it, it was through the act of sacrificial worship that the relationship between men and their pagan gods seems mostly to have been sustained—sacrifices of human beings, horses, dogs, and also of human artefacts such as weapons, tools or boats. Though not, of course, acceptable to the new religion, links could be at least indicated between these and Old Testament sacrificial rites.

More significantly, there was common ground between pagan and Christian feasts. Viking sacrifices seem usually to have been accompanied by a cult feast or orgy at which its members would celebrate with food, drink and sex both the divinity of the god and their own human solidarity and fraternity; and in the course of time it would not be too difficult for the missionaries to transform these feasts into the ale-feasts, church-ales and periodic festive gatherings of the medieval parish or even perhaps to link them with the communion supper central to Christian worship.

As always, the Church had taken superstition and pagan practices into its own service—and after their late acceptance of it the Vikings adopted Christianity with the enthusiasm they brought to all their activities. In Denmark particularly it brought radical changes to the life of the people; from the eleventh to the thirteenth centuries the Danish church was one of the most active in Europe in church building and in its influence on everyday life; as early as 1076 Adam of Bremen describes Skåne as 'now full of churches' (300) with 150 in Zealand and 100 on Funen.

People often ask whether there are any instances of Christianity being clearly seen to alter normal Viking behaviour. One such was the moment when the aged Njal abandons his life-long scheming and resigns himself to the sacrifice of his family in the fire at Bergthorsknoll: 'Be of good heart and speak no words of fear, for this is just a passing storm, and it will be long before another like it comes. Put your faith in the mercy of God for He will not let us burn in this world and the next'.

Since it was so much at variance with the socially approved Viking code of honour and revenge the teaching of forgiveness of one's enemies and the turning of the other cheek must have been one of the least acceptable parts of Christian doctrine, but the seeds of it were there: Gunnar, the very prototype of Viking heroism is forced into fighting (and killing) eight men— 'but I wish I knew whether I am any the less manly than other men for being so much more reluctant to kill than they are?'

Christianity became the accepted religion of Ireland from about 450 and of England from 597. Norse settlements in Ireland were converted between about 980 and 1000 and the Danelaw between 870 and 1020. Denmark, Norway, Iceland and the Kiev-Novgorod kingdom followed suit in the late tenth and early eleventh centuries. Sweden had completed the process by the mid-twelfth century. It must be remembered, however, not only that isolated missionaries were successfully at work in most countries from much earlier dates, but that during the period of general conversion in each country there would still exist every degree between Christianity and paganism.

Possibly the change from old to new was not unalloyed gain—it seldom is. Although few would go as far as one Viking apologist ('The introduction of Christianity was the ruin of all their intellectual splendour; the light of Norse imagination refused to burn 'in the dingy lanterns in which the monks proposed to hide it.') it is nevertheless an undeniable fact that the artistic genius of the later Viking world was eventually choked by the Romanesque, just as its literary pre-eminence over the rest of Europe disappeared for ever under the Latin culture of court and cloister.

The runic alphabet

Like Christianity, the west European Roman alphabet took permanent root in Scandinavia during the tenth century and, though not entirely replacing the alphabet already in use, before long became a new factor in Viking civilization. This earlier, runic alphabet or *futhark* (from the first 6 letters of the earliest example found) had served the pagan folk of north-west Europe during the previous millennium; it was, for example used in parts of Britain between the end of the Roman period and the re-introduction of Christianity.

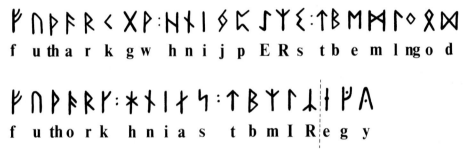

The original futhark (top) and the later form (below).

Runes seem to be derived from one or more of the classic alphabets, such as Etruscan, or possibly from some northern Greek colony, but whatever their origin the shape of the letters had clearly been adapted for easy cutting in wood or stone rather than for use on wax tablets or parchments. Though useful enough for recording names and brief memoranda such as accounts or memorial inscriptions, their paucity and lack of cursive quality did not suit them for any more copious type of literature. Indeed, this was not necessary since from the earliest times the transmission of laws, sagas or poetry had always been quite efficiently taken care of by committing them to the human memory. One code of laws written in runes does exist, but their unsuitability for this or any other literary purpose is nearly as great as the use of Roman numerals in mathematical calculations – e.g. multiplying MCMLXXVI by CCLI!

The full original futhark was in use up to about 700. After this date the 24 letters were modified and contracted to 16. These therefore are the runes actually in use during the Viking period. There is no need to over-stress the magical significance of runes—to the illiterate, reading and writing have at all times been tinged with magic. Nor (because of where so many have chanced to survive) should we deduce that runes were a form of writing specially associated in some way with monumental inscriptions for it is not likely that anyone would learn the art of writing simply in order to carve inscriptions on tombstones! The fact, however, that so many were carved implies that in Viking times there were a fair number of people around sufficiently literate to read them, and indeed it seems not unreasonable to conclude that most Vikings of any standing, or wealth, or of any literary pretensions were probably able to make use of this general-purpose alphabet. That runes were a necessary adjunct to Viking commercial life is indicated by the 550 inscriptions on wood recently excavated in Bergen many of which were to do with trade—millions more wooden ones must have existed and been destroyed over the centuries.

Literature

The runic alphabet was inadequate for a language that, with regional variations, was current all over the Scandinavian world and was the instrument for the greatest outpouring of Nordic literature.

This traditional literature of the Viking world is one of the noblest products of the human spirit during the Dark Ages, but we do well to remind ourselves again of the long time-lag (because of the strength of bardic tradition and inadequacy of runes) between the events or poems and the date when they were actually committed to parchment. The only absolutely contemporary Viking literature is the epigraphic variety, that is, inscriptions on coins or monuments.

The works best known today are the prose sagas (the word means 'something said') rather than the poetry, and of these it is the Icelandic family-sagas which probably appeal to the modern reader rather than the mythical or historical ones. For though there are several valid ways of classifying sagas it is into these three types that they are most conveniently divided. The mythical sagas are those called *lygi* or *fornaldar* sagas—sagas of olden times, based on ancient and widespread traditions. King Hrolf's Saga, *Völsunga Saga* and *Beowulf* are all examples of this type, full of larger-than-life characters all hanging on the merest thread of historical truth; in the whole of *Beowulf* there seems to be only one verifiable event, the fatal raid by king Hygelac on Frisia, which can be tied down to around 521.

The second group of sagas are the historical ones like *Skjöldunga Saga* or the *Ynglinga* and *Sturlunga* sagas and *Heimskringla*, compiled by Snorri Sturluson. Although these are avowedly concerned with the lives of kings and other events in actual time, the modern historian sifts and rejects very thoroughly when quarrying historical material from them. In the words of

170

Styrmir the Learned: 'You can accept from the saga whatever you think most likely, for in these old sagas many things are confused.'

The third section of this saga-literature, and the best known to general readers, comprises the sagas and shorter stories about persons and families, especially in Iceland and the other Atlantic settlements. Many of them have been translated into modern Scandinavian languages and into English and, even though they portray the age to some extent in terms of a later one, nothing recaptures better the atmosphere of the Viking era.

Though not so widely read today, the poetry and verse of the Viking period is quite as remarkable as its prose—again the main source was Iceland where 'poetry was a national industry during the Saga Age and poets a national export'. The output of poetry, 'intoxicating cup of Odin', divides, like the prose, into three classes. At the bottom is the vernacular *hnugg-hent* or 'clipped metre'. Verses of this simple kind were within reach of almost any extempore versifier, such as the servant Narfi in Kormak's Saga, who is boiling sheeps' intestines, 'Kormak, how wouldst thou relish one?—Kettleworms I call them. . . .' Understandably, not much of this humble verse has survived.

Next there is the large body of verse, proverbs and so on, either inserted in the *fornaldar* sagas ('tales of olden time') or forming an independent anthology. Sometimes this verse is called 'eddaic' after the *Edda* of Snorri Sturluson, one of the best known thirteenth-century collections; the *Völuspá* composed in about 1000, is another example. Different metres could be used, including *fornyrdislag* ('the metre of olden time') which was sometimes irregular, or *malahattr* which was normally regular. Much of this poetry was anonymous and traditional like our own Border ballads; other poems were by known authors and composed for specific occasions. A poem can either contain just a few verses (*visur*) or, if at least 20 stanzas long and equipped with refrains, can be dignified by the title of *drapa*. A famous example of verses with a known author and one of the first full-length 'drapas' that has come down to us is the 'Head Ransom' spoken by Egil Skallagrimsson at York in about 948 in the presence of king Eirik Bloodaxe and queen Gunnhild. It is a deliberate eulogy of Eirik by Egil, couched in the most fulsome terms in order to save his own head. A version of the refrains in modern Danish keeps something of the Old Norse metre, and these refrains slip quite easily into English.

Men Erik ry
Sig vandt påny
(But Erik's fame/bathes itself anew)

Gik Erik i land
faldt mangen mand
(Went Erik on land/fell many a man)

But anyone reading eddaic and scaldic verse in the original Old Norse realizes all too soon the virtual impossibility of translating the stanzas themselves. They are so concise and so packed with meaning that an English verse of the same metre and length cannot hope to be adequate; for one thing the brevity of the Old Norse can never be reproduced in a language like ours which requires plentiful prepositions and conjunctions.

The third type of verse recited by the professional bards or scalds was established during the tenth century and was still more rigorously composed. This, 'the glory of Norse metrical art, the stanza form called *drottkvaett*' was specifically composed for recital before the king and his *drott* (entourage). These courtly 'drapas' are often complimentary and ceremonious, their tempo majestic. In form they are even more conventional than eddaic verse, and the conventions are still more exacting. Each stanza has eight lines, and each line is in two halves, with an equal number of syllables and a little pause in the middle—rather as in a sonnet.

The basic unit, the syllable, is normally six to the line (there was a later eight-syllable development). Two lines make a couplet, each of which contains a three-fold alliteration, also a rhyme or half-rhyme, not (as in modern verse) at the end of each line, but inside it. Two couplets complete the half-stanza—the lines themselves can also be linked by alliteration. Once again these verses virtually defy any attempt at exact translation—to maintain the brevity of the metre would mean leaving out half the sense; by abandoning the full meaning one might succeed in retaining the triple stress (perhaps of Celtic origin)—only to sacrifice the alliteration or let go of the rhyme. The following attempt to render in English a stanza from Kormak's Saga gives (inside a hexasyllabic line) some hint of the difficult task the scald was trying to encompass:

> Hail thou hardy sailor
> Hero-poet fearless;
> Loyal lover, royal
> Lord of harp and sword-blade
> Faint the song is flung us
> Far away they harp it
> Crown the warlike Kormak
> King of northern singers.

The metre, rhymes, half-rhymes and alliteration are recognizable, and some of the meaning comes through. But out of its own element every creature is more or less ungainly: the translator of Scandinavian verse faces just the same problems as (for example) a Welshman trying to render *cynghanedd* into English. Literal translation in prose is one way out; here, from *Krákumál* is Ragnar Lodbrok expiring in king Ella's snakepit: 'The bite of vipers is mortal—I feel it invading my breast! My sons will grow pale on

Embracing each other on these little gold foil talismans are ►
perhaps the god Frey and a girl called Gerd he fell in love with.

learning of my death but anger will redden their cheeks again. Such brave warriors will never take their rest until I am avenged in the blood of Ella.'

But with poetry perhaps it is best for every age and tongue to translate freely into its own idiom—certainly some delightfully convincing nineteenth-century renderings of Viking songs have been done in the metre of Meredith's 'Love in a valley', Tennyson's 'Maud' (saying Bright one! my beauty! I love thee. Ah, better by far than my life), even of Longfellow's 'Hiawatha'.

In addition to the metrical exigencies already noted, the scalds (but not usually the eddaic poets) delighted in a number of verbal complexities. Theirs was a crossword-puzzle mentality: periphrastic expressions were their joy, and circumlocution the breath of their poetic life. Their figures of speech, by which many or several words were employed to do the work of one, have been allotted the rather inappropriate term of 'kennings'. Kennings are legion: a sword would become a 'black feathered wound-bird' or the 'wolf of the war-god', a warrior the 'Valkyries tree' or the 'god of the sword', ships 'helm horses' or 'surf deer', and the gallows 'Odin's horses' or the 'wind-cold outcast-tree'. Nor did the game end there. Kennings could be doubled so that a warrior would become the 'god of the black feathered wound-bird'. But the good scald always attempted to develop his metaphors logically and not to mix them, otherwise the verse became 'monstrous'.

Nowhere are the Vikings more explicit about themselves than in that jumble of Icelandic poems known as *Hávamál*, 'The High One's Wisdom', a collection of precepts and proverbs dating from the tenth century. Here are a few of them: 'Never bandy with fools. Never laugh at a hoary counsellor. If you have a trusted friend visit him often: the way no man treads is soon choked with brambles and high grass. Never be the first to break with a friend. It is ill to outrun one's luck. Not many men are brave when they are old if they were cowardly when young. A stout good heart is better than a strong sword—a brave man often wins the day with a blunt blade. Whatever betides him the cheerful man fares better than the whiner. All evils are meted out by fate. Wine is a great wit stealer. If you wish your mistress to yield to you only go to see her at night. Be especially circumspect when you have drunk too much, when you are next to a married woman, when you are among thieves. It is better to have a son late than never; one does not often see memorial stones raised over childless men.'

Like the prose of the sagas, the poetry of the scalds is valuable for its content: for its information on the Norse religion, its social commentary and the light it sheds on the Viking character. But since the beauties and subtleties of its poetical form largely defy translation or paraphrase, enjoyment of the poetry as such is unfortunately restricted to those few who are at home with the Old Norse tongue.

◀ *The stem of the Oseberg ship deeply carved with abstract, intertwining beasts in the earliest Viking decorative style.*

Art and ornament

The impact of the visual arts, on the other hand, is immediate and universal and—up to a point—their appreciation transcends the boundaries imposed by language, time or space.

In general terms, the art styles of western Europe have for many centuries swung between two ideals—ideals which, for want of a better term, we call classical and romantic. The one is governed by strict precepts, is uniform, symmetrical, unchanging, universal in application: the art of the ruler and compass. The other delights in the liberation from exact rules, revels in zoomorphic forms and naturalistic curves, is asymmetrical, individualist: the art of the free hand.

During the Christian era alone, western Europe has seen the pendulum swing a number of times. At the birth of Christ the art of the Celts was still in full flower; its splendid zoomorphic designs dominated every art form. When the Celtic tribes succumbed to the Empire of Rome so did their art; the humble earthenware vessel with its freely modelled hunting scene was soon replaced by the stereotyped product of the Samian-ware factory, stamped with debased classical ornament.

Rome fell: Celtic and Germanic tribal society re-emerged and swamped the classical tradition with a mass of barbaric abstract patterns. After 800 Charlemagne stemmed the tide with his new Roman Empire and the transmuted classicism of Carolingian art gradually re-imposed its discipline on the art and architecture of western Europe.

But Ireland and Scandinavia remained outside, developing—and eventually mingling—their own anti-classical traditions: *Viking Art was the result.* In England the Anglo-Saxon artists mastered Carolingian and successfully fused it with their own barbaric heritage: there the 'Winchester' style was born.

The heir to Carolingian classical was Romanesque (a nineteenth-century general term). By the twelfth century, Romanesque had mopped up the remnants of the 'barbaric' animal art over most of western Europe – Scandinavia held out the longest.

Scandinavian art of the Viking age had its roots in the continental German tradition of barbaric ornament and hatred of naturalistic treatment. It consistently avoided straight lines, right angles and repetitive ornament, all essential to classical art. But it diverged very early on from the German tradition in one significant respect – a devotion to animal rather than plant motifs. Once this separation had been achieved, styles in art in Scandinavia became, like religion and language, homogenous over the whole area.

That art, or rather ornament, was very much a part of the Viking's daily life is clear from its occurrence on all kinds of everyday object. However much we may esteem some of its aspects we should not be deluded into uncritical admiration of everything the Viking age produced. Form and line, particularly in the earlier periods, are sacrificed to ornament which is flashy and repetitive.

Viking decorative style contemporary with the earliest Viking raids represented the latest stage of a centuries-old tradition of ornament based on animal and human forms. As always with anti-classical artists, these forms were distorted (often beyond recognition), jumbled up and re-used as ingredients for new, abstract designs—Celtic artists 900 years earlier had similarly reduced the triumphal Greek chariot and horses on a Greek stater to a mish-mash of limbs and wheels.

It was not that the northern peoples were unable to create naturalistic art—the Gotland picture stones and random examples that have survived from elsewhere disprove this—they simply preferred their own intimate subjective vision. Sometimes this was highly individualist and sophisticated and produced the extraordinary little creatures seen in the metal bridle-mounts from Broa in Sweden. In the same style, known as Salin Style III, is the carved woodwork on the famous ship from Oseberg in Norway, though the wagon from there also has semi-naturalistic figures. Many of the abstract figures in Style III grip themselves or each other with their paws.

This 'gripping beast' also features in the next style, which is named from Borre, near Oseberg. A second motif in the Borre style is a leonine animal composed of ogee curves and spirals with a distinctive, backward-looking head. But it is a third element by which the Borre style is most easily recognized. This consists of interlacing patterns of ribbon and cord or of straps, plaits and 'ring-chain'; it occurs all over Viking Scandinavia, and is particularly common in the Isle of Man and the Danelaw on monuments such as crosses and hog-back tombs. The Borre style also appears in Sweden and the East—it is typified in a massive silver brooch found in the Voronezh district of Russia.

The Borre style and the Jelling and the Mammen styles are all closely related and overlap each other in the date and appearance of their artefacts. Together they dominate the main central period of Viking activity and settlement. The two new ones take their names from places in Jutland. Jelling is now just a village but in the mid-tenth century it was a focal point in the Danish state, seat of her powerful line of kings and perhaps also an artistic centre. In the Jelling and Mammen styles, the lion-like Borre animal retains his spiral hip but has also borrowed the ribbon motif and grown himself an elongated, sinuous ribbon- or strap-work body which often symmetrically intertwines with another beast of the same shape. It is thus that he appears on a silver cup from Jelling and in majestic form on the Jelling stone. He is the direct ancestor of the 'Great Beast' who, with or without accompanying snake, dominates the art of Scandinavia during its last two periods.

This new elongated animal introduces a fresh element of graceful linear draughtsmanship, and a decorated battle-axe from Mammen shows full

Viking decorative style contemporary with
the earliest raids had its roots in the
abstract, animal designs of the Celts (top
left) and appears in an individual and
sophisticated form on a bronze bridle-
mount from Broa (top centre). The wagon
end from Oseberg (left centre) is of the
same period and the same sinuousness but
is more representational, perhaps illustrating a heroic story.

Intertwining legs and bodies become
interlacing ribbons in the Borre style, here
seen on three tombs in a church in Viking
Northumbria (below left). But a beast with
a backward-turning head was another
Borre characteristic and that reappears in
Mammen and Ringerike designs (the great
axe from Mammen is at top right). Ringerike was much favoured in England and
Ireland where the beasts acquired a more
naturalistic air and were caught up in
plant-like tendrils (below right).

The Jelling style, another development
from Borre, was not only copied in England but was returned to Scandinavia as
an English idiosyncrasy.

Picture stones in Gotland, sometimes
standing as much as 12 feet high (below
centre), are purely representational—a
rare phenomenon in Viking art.

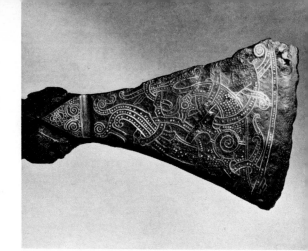

mastery of the style by fitting it into an awkward space. There is also complete self-assurance, and combination of the practical and aesthetic, in the gilt bronze fittings from a pair of harness bows found at Søllested on the island of Funen. But both axe and harness bows show how foliage is now creeping into the hitherto exclusively animal ornament—leafy tendrils and scrolls which, like the repetitive beaded borders have been borrowed from the Carolingian style then prevalent in western Europe.

This prompts the question: 'By the late tenth century how much were artistic influences flowing into the Scandinavian homelands from those countries which the Vikings raided or settled?' Such impressionable and adaptable people could hardly remain uninfluenced by the art forms they found in England, Ireland or Normandy and in fact a continuous feed-back had been taking place from the ninth century. The close contacts between Ireland and Norway make the relationship between Irish and Scandinavian art a certainty, particularly in the field of woodcarving, and on metal objects likewise there is a fertilization of Scandinavian art by Irish which reaches its full flower in the eleventh and twelfth centuries when Irish carvings and even Irish manuscript illuminations are imbued with Scandinavian elements.

Much of the early stimulus—that is from Ireland to Scandinavia—will have come through a highly portable form of loot, the manuscript gospels and psalters executed by Irish monks during the ninth and tenth centuries. Though the Vikings no doubt destroyed many books they did bring back to Norway and Denmark numbers of rolled up pages of illuminated vellum from them whose design and decoration would influence Scandinavian craftsmen. The gold and gilt-bronze ornaments ripped off the bindings of these books were great favourites with Viking women, being of a convenient size for mounting as brooches; they will have had a direct influence on Scandinavian metalwork.

The Jelling and related styles may however have been influenced not only by direct 'borrowing' from Ireland but also by the synthesizing and maturing of Irish and Scandinavian styles in the halfway houses of the Isle of Man and the northern Danelaw. This accounts for the similarities—for example, sharp angles and double lappets—between Jelling-style metalwork in Scandinavia and its stone counterpart in Britain: the decoration of the Søllested harness bows is echoed in a Manx stone cross.

The nameplace of the next style is the prosperous farming district north of Oslo called Ringerike. By now, plant ornament, in particular that derived from the classical acanthus, has almost driven out animal ornament. Animals, especially the 'Great Beast' himself, are now represented as substantial creatures and in a fairly naturalistic manner (though they still tend to retain the Style III spiral at their hip-joints). In the Ringerike style they no longer appear just as a means—a source of ornamental ingredients— but as an end in themselves. The 'Great Beast' is caught up in the scrolls, tendrils and acanthus leaves sprouting from his own ears and tail.

The nearest approach to the representational made by the main stream of Scandinavian art are the Gotland picture-stones: numerous sandstone and limestone monuments from that island, many of which are carved—presumably as memorials—with bas-relief scenes depicting Viking life and mythology. The picture comes first and mere ornament is secondary. They form a unique and valuable source of information on the appearance of people, animals, weapons, cult-scenes and especially of the Viking warriors' most treasured possession—ships. They date from well before Viking times through to the end of the eleventh century.

When upright, the tallest stones were 12 feet high, their most characteristic shape being a keyhole or—surely more plausibly—an erect phallus. Indeed they may very well represent the *flannstaungr*, or penis-poles, whose erection was one of the things banned by the early Christian church.

We now come to the last and arguably the most splendid manifestation of art during the Viking period, named after the decoration in the church of the little village of Urnes in Norway. The Urnes style is a recognizable sequel to that of Ringerike, for the 'Great Beast' and the serpent, both enmeshed in tendrils and foliage, still pursue their pattern as before. But the execution in this brilliant final flowering of Scandinavian art has become refreshingly and astonishingly different. All the forms are thinned and refined, so that the open and boldly planned interlacing animal limbs are inextricably blended with the snake coils and plant foliage.

The result is a fantasia whose grace surpasses all the previous ribbon styles and semi-barbaric ornament. As Dr. Shetelig says, the new taste 'aimed at something clearer and simpler than the rich and crowded effect of the Jelling decorations . . . in contrast with the dense and strictly symmetrical effect of the Jelling interlacings the Urnes decorations are designed in graceful curves as free and open compositions'.

The wooden doorframe and west gable panel from this remote little Norwegian church illustrates the one brief occasion when the art of Viking Scandinavia stands unquestionably on an equal footing with anything the rest of the world has produced. For a brief occasion it was; because this brilliant final flowering of indigenous Nordic art took place just at the inauspicious moment when the abilities of northern artists and architects were being engulfed by the all-embracing Romanesque.

That it can be successfully translated from wood to metal, and from architectural carving down to small objects, are tests of its integrity as a style; the Urnes idiom of scroll and interlace is particularly pleasing in bronze, openwork ornaments from Norway and England and in a silver brooch from Lindholm Høje in Denmark. With their beautifully balanced asymmetry these pieces anticipate the flowing line and intricacy of form associated with the anti-classical art of a much later age—the 'rococo' styles

181

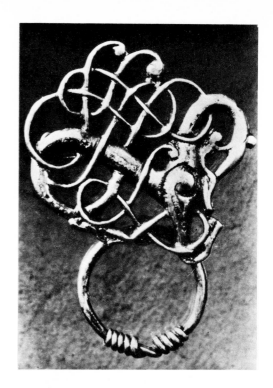

The peak of achievement in Viking art is named after the embellishments of the church at Urnes in Norway (left). It is a fined-down, boldly executed version of all the foregoing beasts and tendrils, with flowing lines that are assymetrically pleasing in a brooch from Lindholm Høje (above) that has much of the 18th-century Rococo about it (above left).

of eighteenth-century Europe and particularly of England between 1745 and 1760.

Within its limited world (Britain and Scandinavia) the Urnes idiom was recognized during the eleventh and twelfth centuries as the accepted vehicle for orthodox Christian art. Kirkburn in the East Riding is almost as remote a church as Urnes itself, but the capitals there are unmistakably sculptured with Urnes ornament; until replaced by later rebuilding many other examples must have existed. (Urnes is one of many stave churches in Norway, but Greenstead [Essex] is the only one to survive in England.) However, the total dedication of the Norman conquerors to provincial Romanesque meant that architectural decoration like this could not survive for long even in the Danelaw and traces of it after about 1100 are hard to find. It is a curious paradox that what must have been one of the latest examples of the Urnes style in England is the crosier of that arch-Norman bishop of Durham, Ranulf Flambard.

Ireland, on the other hand, was spared a Norman invasion until 1169 and during this century of grace, design continued to be influenced by the art of Scandinavia, some of it of the earlier Jelling style but most of it Urnes in character. Indeed the century and a half between the battle of Clontarf (1014) and the Plantagenet invasions provided a long period of growth and synthesis which produced such splendid works as the Clonmacnois abbot's crosier and the stone sarcophagus from Cashel.

Some confusion may arise from the Urnes style having sometimes been called 'the rune-stone-style' because of the huge number of stones and rockfaces—mostly memorials—in Sweden, Öland and Gotland carved and painted by eleventh-century artists who used the figures of eight and serpentine convolutions as the vehicle for their runic inscriptions. At times these rune-stone designs are highly sophisticated, at others degenerate; sometimes they occur with Ringerike overtones.

Viking ships

Occasionally a human device—a means—is so perfectly contrived that it becomes a work of art, that is, an end, in itself. In all the other methods of transport—they had carts, wagons, sledges, skis and skates—the Vikings were no more than ordinarily competent—indeed their wheel construction was rather more primitive than elsewhere. But their ships were another matter, and since without the peculiar perfection of these vessels the whole seething upsurging manifestation of sheer energy which we call the Viking movement would probably have boiled itself away inside Scandinavia the ship has rightly been accepted as a symbol of the Viking age.

How did the Vikings manage to be so much ahead of their more southerly neighbours in the matter of shipbuilding? There is without much doubt a historical connection between the ships that the tribes on the Baltic possessed in the days of Tacitus, and those developed by the Vikings. In other words the art of shipbuilding had a longer tradition and was better preserved in Scandinavia than elsewhere in northern Europe; this is not surprising when we remember that the Vikings excelled all their neighbours in the art of working timber.

Their other excellence lay in the development of a particular and unique design. Unlike everybody else's vessels the Vikings' succeeded by virtue of being a complete contradiction in terms; they were really sailing canoes. Because a seventy-foot Viking vessel drew only two or three feet of water it could sail much faster than any conventional ship of similar length which might draw up to ten feet. Secondly, the sides of these 'canoes'—and this applies even to the great longships—were low enough for their crews to use oars. Thirdly without the drag of a keeled vessel they were relatively easy to row when the wind failed.

They have also been paradoxically nicknamed 'ocean-going landing craft' and this quality gave their Viking users the enormous advantage of sailing much farther into shallow rivers and estuaries and the ability to land there. On isolated shores without harbours ships drawing ten feet of water were useless when it came to putting men or horses ashore. Viking vessels could be beached on any sandy shallow bay whether in the Orkneys or Lindisfarne, Thanet or Sheppey, Jeufosse in the Seine or Noirmoutier in the Loire. Indeed, because these are generally inaccessible from attack by other sea-goers, the Vikings deliberately chose shallow waters in preference to conventional harbours. The Bayeux tapestry shows the Viking ship's immense advantage for unloading horses.

Often as she has been subsequently described, there is still a fascination in the account of the Gokstad ship's first excavation in 1880. 'The vessel was seventy-eight foot long and seventeen foot at the widest part; five foot nine inches from keel to gunwale and probably drawing three foot of water. She had twenty ribs and was clinker-built. The planks and timbers of the frame were fastened with withies or roots: the timbers seem to be naturally grown and not artificially bent. The boards of the side were about one and a half inches thick, of well-seasoned oak, smoothly planed and fastened with iron rivets, clenched in each side, also with oaken bolts near the upper parts. Bow and stern were the same shape, pointed, and rising for a considerable distance out of the water. The keel was deep, and made of thick oaken beams. The flooring could be lifted out in order to bail out the ship. Decks and rowers' seats had been removed for the burial. The rudder was a large oar consisting of blade with short handle fixed about two feet from the stern to a piece of conical wood projecting about a foot from the vessel. The steering was effected by a tiller fixed in a hole in the upper end of the handle. The vessel had one mast.'

One Viking ship which seems to have been rather forgotten since her discovery in 1878 is the vessel found at the mouth of the Monmouthshire

Perhaps their ships are the Vikings' best known works of art. Grace of line and elegance of detail were combined in their design with a consideration for their purpose that was un-surpassed at the time. They were ocean-going landing craft, as the Bayeux Tap-estry shows (above) ef-ficiently equipped as well as beautiful (the Oseberg anchor, below, is still com-plete with rings for cable and buoy rope).

185

Usk. She was lightly built, of clinker construction, in Danzig oak (less hard and compact than English oak). She was caulked with wool or sheepskins and fastened with nails and trenails. She was seventy foot long, with a beam of twenty foot and seems to have had some sort of deck—apparently the only Viking *langskib* ever found in the British Isles. 'They built great ships and sailed them.' John Masefield's epitaph on the Victorians can be applied with equal force to the Vikings.

Chapter VIII   The Viking Legacy

According to his habits, the present reader has dipped, skipped, looked at the pictures, thumbed the index, or plodded patiently through the preceding chapters, where yet another attempt has been made to glimpse the Vikings in their own time—time past. But before this latest account is concluded and added to the stack it does seem worth while looking at the Viking phenomenon from our own time—time present—and asking what it is about this particular episode in European history that has aroused an interest so sustained, and so apparently disproportionate to the numbers of human beings actually involved.

Unquestionably, Viking settlements in western Europe from around 800 to 1100 did have significance for the subsequent histories of the countries concerned. But the fact remains that numerically these settlements were insignificant compared, for example, with the vast emigration from Europe to North America that took place a millennium later, when, between about 1860 and 1920 (a much shorter period), some 52 million people crossed the Atlantic—among them 300,000 Danes and a proportionate number of Norwegians and Swedes.

Yet this vast and mainly peaceful settlement has not attracted a tithe of the attention accorded to the comparatively tiny migrations of the Vikings. Is our clue here this word 'peaceful?' Is it the (supposedly) extra-bloodthirsty character of the Viking expansion that has confused our perspective and blown up into an epic what was 'no more than an episode . . . in the great human adventure'? (A comparable instance is of course the American 'Western' where, in response to popular demand, the film industry has reared an enormous superstructure of fiction and romance on a limited, and frequently sordid, basis of fact.)

The answer to these questions must be a qualified yes. For had the Viking emigrants been required by some historical legerdemain to conform to the procedures of their nineteenth- and twentieth-century successors—

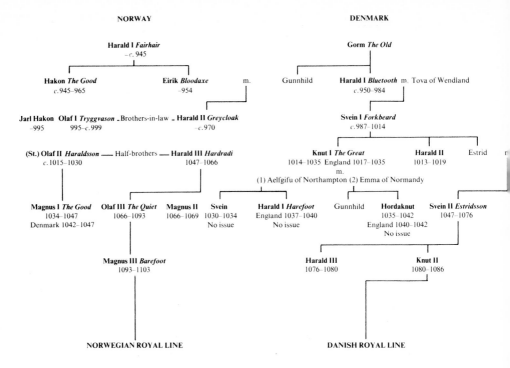

The Viking ancestry of four of the main ruling houses of Europe.

passports, steamship tickets, customs, immigration permits and so on—they might have been applauded for their industry in settling new lands, but their 'Press' would have been non-existent.

Equally, if the Vikings' trading activities had always been conducted in an orderly and peaceable fashion they would never have hit the contemporary headlines; their notoriety, like that of Hawkins and Drake in Elizabethan times, was partly the result of the facility with which they were able to switch from trading to raiding and from commerce to piracy. A Viking merchant from Kildale (N. Yorkshire) was buried with his scales and weights—but also with his sword and dagger!

Is it then the Viking qualities of independence, pragmatism and initiative that have excited the interest and perhaps envy of the later twentieth century? It is no coincidence that the generations which have idolized movie-stars of the 'Westerns' are the same ones that have acclaimed the Vikings, and for the same reasons: the unquenchable thirst of this age for vicarious experience and excitement and for heroes who, in contrast to the common lot, stand and fall, like the ancient Greeks, by their own courage.

Up till the appearance of P. B. du Chaillu's *Viking Age* in 1889, Danes, Norwegians and Swedes had always been referred to in history under their own prosaic nationalities, or under the anonymous cover of 'Scandinavian Antiquities'. The only hint of romance was in the generic term 'Northmen'

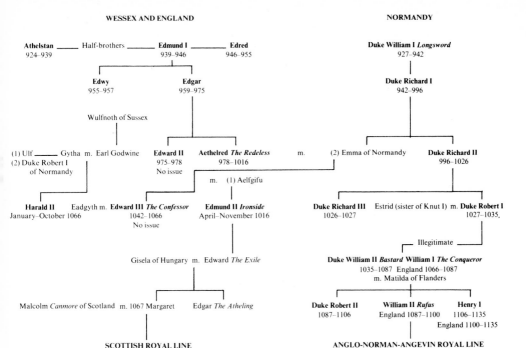

Athelstan ———— Half-brothers ———— **Edmund I** ———— **Edred**
924–939   939–946   946–955

Duke William I *Longsword*
927–942

Edwy   **Edgar**
955–957   959–975

Duke Richard I
942–996

Wulfnoth of Sussex

(1) Ulf ———— Gytha m. Earl Godwine   **Edward II**   **Aethelred** *The Redeless*   m.   (2) **Emma of Normandy**   **Duke Richard II**
(2) Duke Robert I   975–978   978–1016   996–1026
   of Normandy   No issue

m.   (1) Aelfgifu

Harald II   Eadgyth m. **Edward III** *The Confessor*   **Edmund II** *Ironside*   **Duke Richard III**   Estrid (sister of Knut I) m. **Duke Robert I**
January–October 1066   1042–1066   April–November 1016   1026–1027   1027–1035,
                  No issue

Illegitimate

Gisela of Hungary m. Edward *The Exile*   **Duke William II** *Bastard* **William I** *The Conqueror*
                                                             1035–1087 England 1066–1087
                                                               m. Matilda of Flanders

Malcolm *Canmore* of Scotland   m. 1067 Margaret   Edgar *The Atheling*   **Duke Robert II**   **William II** *Rufus*   **Henry I**
                                                          1087–1106   England 1087–1100   1106–1135
                                                                                          England 1100–1135

SCOTTISH ROYAL LINE   **ANGLO-NORMAN-ANGEVIN ROYAL LINE**

(Normannerne), the name used by Johannes Steenstrup in the greatest of all early accounts of the Vikings, published in Copenhagen between 1876 and 1882.

Since the beginning of this century, however, scarcely a year has passed without the appearance of one or more general studies of the Vikings by that name; together with a string of works on various particular aspects of their history and literature. Once again the question arises: 'Why this profusion?' but this time our explanation must seek to go deeper than the superficial or emotional reasons, and try to discover if there is something that people of subsequent ages have found in the Viking age which responds to their more fundamental needs and aspirations, or maybe can be shown to have actually influenced the societies in which they live.

Democracy

In western Europe over the past nine centuries the relationship of the common man—the freeman—with his social and political organization has undergone many ups and downs. His share in the government of his country has fluctuated from people to people and century to century. There have been all-too-numerous periods of profound dissatisfaction, culminating in strikes, civil war and revolution.

A biographer is always to some degree his subjects' advocate, and the writer of a book on the Vikings must therefore beware of attributing all democratic trends—personal liberty, freedom of opinion, active participation in government and so on—solely to the Scandinavian legacy in the countries they occupied. Even in Iceland and Scandinavia itself, unconquered and relatively free from outside influence though they have been, a continuous record of democracy has not been achieved.

Still, compared with the rest of continental Europe, their record has been quite an impressive one. Iceland has held its Althing parliament continuously since the tenth century. In Denmark from 1282 there have been annual meetings of a parliamentary institution—the *Hof*, later *Danehof* and *Rigsdag* alongside and often in opposition to the royal power. All attempts to foist Roman and German law on the Danish people failed; not only did Danish law remain free from foreign influence, and written in Danish not Latin, but in the old Viking tradition there was never a moment when the people were denied the right to make laws. In Sweden there has been a continuous parliament (*Riskdag*) with representatives from the 'three estates' since 1435. In short, the northern tradition of freedom, though it may have sometimes gone underground, always re-emerged and neither in the eleventh century nor in subsequent ones did feudalism ever get a real foothold in Scandinavia. One reason was that the extraction of Britain from Scandinavia in 1066 removed Scandinavia from European influences.

Since the Middle Ages, although there have been frequent reactionary eddies in Denmark and Sweden and the countries they ruled (Norway till 1905, Iceland till 1944), the main tide has continued to flow steadily in the traditions of democracy. By the nineteenth and twentieth centuries these traditions and all that goes with them had been firmly established under a series of mainly liberal and social democratic governments. Shamefully ignorant though we British are of our Scandinavian neighbours most of us are at least aware of their outstanding achievement in such matters as education, land tenure, social services, labour relations and the welfare of the common man.

For a number of reasons our own British story is a far more complicated one, and in the present context can only be outlined—naturally at some risk of over-simplification: One way through the labyrinth is to try and unravel the silken thread of personal liberty from the cords of 'feudalism'.

As we saw, the Norman conquest wrenched England (and eventually the whole of Britain) from Viking Scandinavia and shackled her enduringly to the European continent. It would be foolish to deny the long-term cultural gains conferred on Britain by this long-deferred link-up with the riches of the Mediterranean culture, or the economic wealth which would come through her trade across the narrow seas. But the political gains of this earlier 'entry into Europe' are a much more debatable matter, and whatever we may think about feudalism it can hardly be denied that it was a

190

Ship-burial, by burning the dead man with his ship or interring ►
them in a mound, did not survive into Christian times.

misfortune for England that it should have to be introduced by the Normans, who, of all west European peoples, were the closest to the barbarian strain.

Regrets aside, it is a matter for surprise that in the 1060s the Normans, instead of conquering England, did not turn their energies against the neighbouring and already feudalized kingdom of France. England and Scandinavia might then have had the chance of integrating gradually with Europe with the bonds between them remaining unbroken and the common Nordic traditions of liberty developing undisturbed. As for France, under efficient Norman rule she would probably have been spared the intermittent anarchy which she was due to suffer during the next four centuries!

As it was, to almost every free Englishman living from the accession of king Edward (1043) to the death of king William (1087) the Norman conquest must have brought some diminution of rights; to many it will have seemed an unqualified disaster. For, whether of Saxon, Anglian, Danish or Norwegian descent Englishmen now suddenly became the subjects of a foreign despot and (most of them) the underdogs of a foreign aristocracy.

Norman feudalism has aroused some strong feelings among our Whig historians: 'a weed of rank growth, unfitted to the interests and almost to the instincts of Englishmen'; 'utterly subversive of liberty and unfavourable to the best interests of society'; 'the medium through which the various and disgusting forms of arbitrary domination were established' . . . and so on.

It has also been an article of faith with these historians that after the Norman conquest a substantial body of Englishmen survived, detesting feudalism and all that it stood for; and that after long and arduous struggles these freedom-fighters eventually rendered the hated system inoperative (late fifteenth century), abolished it from the statute-book (mid-seventeenth century) and finally destroyed it for ever in the Glorious Revolution of 1688, since when we should all have lived happily ever after. . . .

The horrors of the twentieth century, with tyranny and inhumanity more widespread and fearful than anything the feudal age could encompass have effectively discredited much of the liberal progressivists' view of history. But one part of their thesis does stand. The survival of a large and prosperous area of post-conquest England, containing a relatively free population is a plain historical fact. That area is the Danelaw, especially the northern Danelaw: Lincolnshire and (after its recovery from the devastation of 1069) Yorkshire. Its inhabitants are the men and women of Anglo-Viking, that is, virtually unmixed Scandinavian stock, whose story we followed in chapters III and IV. In chapter IV we saw how important place-name evidence is for our knowledge of the Danelaw settlement, especially because of the relative deficiency of material evidence like coins, inscriptions or buildings.

However, besides place-names there does exist other non-material evidence, and some of it has been extensively explored during this century;

◄ *A Viking brooch in bronze, sheet-silver and black niello.*   193

family and personal names have been studied, comparative philology has been applied to surviving dialects; folklore, folk-life and folk customs and superstitions in Scandinavia and the Danelaw have been compared.

But, as Professor Kendrick has rightly pointed out: 'The memorial to the Vikings in the British Isles is more than a parcel of names and a few fossil customs.' There is a still further body of non-material evidence from which their real legacy will gradually be revealed—their contributions to the basic structure of English society, to the legal system, to the administration of justice and perhaps to the very character and physique of the northern Englishman and woman.

Over a century ago Danish historians like Worsaae and Steenstrup gave convincing proofs of the existence of this evidence, and since then the unique attributes of the Danelaw have been examined by a number of Danish and English historians. In his *Anglo-Saxon England, The Danes in England*, and other authoritative works, Professor F. M. Stenton has explored more deeply than any other historian the survival into the Middle Ages and beyond of Viking descendants, living in villages independent of the organization of the manor, holding their lands by payment of rent rather than by services, securing the issue of their own writs of right, issuing their own charters, responsible for the payment of their own taxes, and generally enjoying 'a measure of freedom quite unparalleled in the south and west of the country'.

Professor Stenton is also one of the foremost to point out that the strength of the Scandinavian evidence has still been underestimated; partly because of its tenuous and imponderable qualities it has not yet been adequately followed up by researchers or given sufficient weight by conventional historians. As the Vikings' advocate and apologist it is not unreasonable at least to suggest that we may discover in their character the source of some of the tolerance, cooperative spirit and respect for the individual which has long characterized western liberalism and remind ourselves once more that the English parliamentary and jury systems are the fruits not of Norman but of Anglo-Scandinavian initiatives.

In the later twentieth century we are all increasingly conscious of England's north/south dichotomy. 'England, God knows, is culturally divided', wrote a recent reviewer, 'The Trent is a frontier that separates two distinct countries.' Geographically, a more accurate assessment is the 'Potter's Bar syndrome' so widespread among southerners, who view with suspicion (or completely ignore) all points north and east of the Home Counties! Without any doubt what we have here, preserved like flies in amber, are the old Saxon attitudes of fear, envy and distrust of territory neighbouring yet distinct, whose inhabitants' ways of life and thought still reflect an ancient and freer past.

The large number of *liberi homines*—free men—surviving in the Danelaw up to the date of Magna Carta (1215) and into the reigns of Henry

III and Edward I were well placed for subsequent social and economic development. From the fourteenth century until the eighteenth subsidy rolls and other documents reveal that this part of England supported an exceptionally strong body of prosperous yeomen and minor gentry (the two were often inter-married and virtually indistinguishable) farming their own modest estates and leading the kind of life not so very different from the *holds*, *thegns* and *drengs* of Viking times—indeed in Northumbria there was a survival of these two latter terms. Moreover, even up to the second half of the nineteenth century it was still possible to distinguish at least in Lincolnshire a body of smaller freehold proprietors surviving to an extent unknown in the rest of England, alongside the normal ranks of the squirearchy and 'bourgeoisie'.

Language

There is no doubt about the massive Scandinavian influence on the English language. The language of the Danelaw remained basically Norse well into the Middle Ages; further north, in the Orkneys, a Scandinavian speech called 'Norn' was the common tongue until the end of the eighteenth century. To this day the Anglo-Scandinavian dialects spoken in eastern England still have a very strong affinity, both in their vocabulary and pronunciation, with old Scandinavian—an affinity not shared by the dialects spoken in southern England.

Because these latter are direct descendants of the 'English' of Alfred the Great it is often assumed that the speech of Wessex was the true ancestor of modern English. But this is not so: the speech of king Alfred is represented today by the dialects of 'Zummerzet' and neighbouring counties, and the dialect groups from which modern English mainly derives are those originally current in Northumbria and eastern Mercia, areas of the Danelaw. We say 'originally' because the boundaries of dialect groups, and therefore of the individual words belonging to them, have never remained static. Many words and features of the language that were previously just Anglian or Scandinavian have gradually moved southward and affected the dialect of London, the immediate ancestor of modern English. 'Them', 'their', 'take', 'eggs' have gradually replaced the Saxon *hem*, *hir*, *niman*, *eyren*. 'Many names there are in England in the *Norræna* tongue', says *Heimskringla*. But this name evidence is reinforced by an abundance of ordinary words used in modern 'standard' English: law, by-law (the law of the *by*, commonly misspelt bye-law), fellow, skull, skin, sky (which in modern Scandinavian only means cloud!), window, birth, thrift—all these and many more come directly from the Old Norse. Modern Danelaw dialects use of course far more Scandinavian words: teem (pour), lake (play), addle (earn), flit (move house), gaumless (foolish) and stee (ladder) are only half a dozen out of hundreds in daily use.

Two of the reasons why English, once an obscure local dialect in a remote little island, has become the world language it is today are directly traceable to the fact that its principal sources happened to lie in the Anglo-Scandinavian portion of that island rather than its West Saxon, Teutonic area. This geographical factor has conferred on English first, a comparative simplicity of grammar, and second, a matchless vocabulary, a real 'treasury of words'. The former results from a virtual absence of genders, cases and inflections (for example an easy-to-remember 's' forms the plural of most nouns and a simple 'ed' the past tense of most weak verbs). This tendency to discard inflections and so on, showed itself very early in the Anglian dialects of the North, whereas those of Wessex tended to retain them. Had the latter won the day modern English might have been as cluttered with inflexions as modern German.

As to vocabulary, Anglian Northumbria back in the days of Bede had been the first region to produce a literary culture and on to this native lexicon the Danish and Norwegian invasions of the ninth and tenth centuries grafted a large number of additional Norse words—the two tongues, Northumbrian and Old Norse were near enough to each other for a mutual assimilation and enrichment to take place, from which many additional words eventually entered standard English.

In addition to this legacy of linguistic riches there has been a relatively strong survival in Britain of customs, traditions, superstitions, childrens' games (these latter have an enormous survival power) which are directly traceable to Viking influence. Naturally this is more pronounced in the old Danelaw areas than elsewhere in the country.

Character

Enough has been said to establish the Scandinavian share in the making of that beautiful and complex musical instrument, the English language. The Viking influence on the English character is more subtle and imponderable and we can do no more here than throw out a few hints and comparisons. The difficulty is not so much with the Viking character and outlook—these come over for the most part loud and clear. It is due much more to the impossibility of arriving at a generally acceptable analysis of a present-day Englishman without plunging into a mass of subjective judgements and unprofitable generalizations.

One could, for instance, draw a plausible comparison between generally accepted Viking attributes and attitudes and those of (say) a Cumbrian farmer or a Flamborough fisherman; but the likenesses become less recognizable in the case of an elderly rentier from Bournemouth or an unemployed immigrant in Brixton.

Although there is always a gap between the actual and the ideal, the characteristics on which the English have so often ideally prided themselves fit the Viking mould rather well: a sturdy, hard-working, law-loving people, fond of good cheer and strong drink, of shrewd blunt speech and a stubborn reticence when speech would be useless or foolish; a people faithful to friend and kinsman, truthful, hospitable, liking to make a fair show but not vain or boastful, a people with perhaps little play of fancy or great range of imagination, but cool-thinking, resolute, determined, able to face danger without fuss and to realize the plain facts of life clearly and even deeply, a people with a healthy independence, originality and sense of humour.

Other traditionally 'English' qualities which spring to mind as common both to them and to their Viking forebears are those active virtues summed up in the Scandinavian adjective *driftig*—initiative, ambition, willpower, zest for conquest and adventure, together with self-help, enterprise, and industry. That these qualities were still held in esteem up to the earlier part of this century is evident from the popularity of English writers like William Cobbett, Samuel Smiles and John Ruskin.

To enquire how we in the twentieth century's last quarter measure up to the qualities listed above might appear irrelevant to this book were it not that so many present trends lead so consistently in the opposite direction that they seem to form a veritable present-day pattern of 'anti-Vikingism'. For example the Vikings were men of action; they made decisions and acted on them according to the needs of the hour, they were active, practical, pragmatic. So, until recent decades were the English, who were famed (and sometimes derided) for their down-to-earth, business-like approach to every situation. But since 1945 or is it 1918?—England has become obsessed with self-conscious theorizing and philosophizing; and the tendency to think or write about doing something rather than actually do it.

The Vikings were eminently common-sensible; they believed the evidence of their own eyes and other senses. The English have latterly all too often abandoned their natural sagacity in favour of statistical and computerized information, frequently extrapolated from unsound original premises with disastrously inaccurate results.

Both in war and trade the Vikings attached great importance to the formation by free men of a variety of partnerships and fellowships; the very word 'fellow' comes from Old Norse *felag* meaning a partner. For centuries the English have been particularly good at forming free association groups of all kinds, guilds and fellowships, whether religious or mercantile, clubs, associations, institutes, societies and voluntary organizations supporting a legion of social and charitable causes. These performed a huge variety of productive tasks and welfare activities at almost no expense to the state and with a healthy independence of state authority.

Since 1906, and still more since 1945, English social legislation and state organization have provided an all-embracing system of education and welfare. This has performed miracles for the material well-being of her population but has also made much of the old voluntary spirit redundant.

The Viking image was still strong in the mind of the man who made this chess piece in the Hebrides in the 12th century, islands taken over by the Norwegians early in the Viking era and remaining under Norse rule after the Norman conquest of England.

Without perhaps intending to, the welfare state has sapped some of our traditional self-reliance and enterprise—we are better cared for but less *driftig* than formerly. Moreover, the system has only been achieved by huge and often wasteful expenditure on the part of central and local government, and by the setting up of an enormous bureaucracy.

As human types, the Viking and the bureaucrat are about as far apart as it is possible to get; in the time that the one has translated thought into action the other has dictated a memo. Indeed, in the bureaucratic mind the issuing of a piece of paper has frequently become a substitute for the carrying out of the actual job.

Viking men and women could hardly have faced their usually difficult and dangerous lives without a high degree of self-confidence. For centuries this has been a traditionally English quality too, and one by no means unknown among English civil servants, particularly during the great Liberal administrations of the nineteenth and early twentieth centuries.

But what one now senses is a loss of confidence; a loss which may well be linked with that other appalling deprivation—two generations of her best citizens—that England has suffered since 1914. Whatever the reasons, bureaucratic decisions which were formerly settled at the appropriate lower level are now often sent all the way up the line, with trivial matters demanding ministerial attention. Natural human lethargy apart, many administrators appear so scared of putting a foot wrong that they rarely put one forward at all. It is a far cry from Viking pragmatism.

As we have seen a man's first loyalties in Viking Scandinavia were to his fellow soldiers and to his kinsmen—the extended family—then towards these same elements in bigger groupings like herreds, hundares and wapentakes, and finally to the larger regional units. And, whatever the century or country, these are the levels rather than the national (or nationalized) ones, which seem to provide the circumstances in which human beings will function at their best with the maximum output both of energy and contentedness.

In fact, neither in Viking times nor subsequently has the northern bent been towards nationalism. The Scandinavian and English parliamentary and jury systems evolved from the northern tradition of moots and things; gatherings small enough for full participation in decision-making by every individual present, and in which those who made the decisions also carried them out.

A freedom tradition survived in England strong enough to destroy in turn Norman feudalism and Tudor/Stuart absolutism. Is some atavistic memory of our Viking heritage behind today's increasing dissatisfaction with too many laws and taxes, too much bureaucracy, people's growing conviction that bigger is not better, nor centralization a sound recipe for human happiness? If so, we should hearken to it.

List of illustrations

COLOUR PHOTOGRAPHS

Index